Also by Debra Stark

If Kallimos Had A Chef, VanderWyk & Burnham, 2001
Eat Well Be Happy: A Second Bite, 2004, Debra's Natural Gourmet
The Blue Ribbon Edition: From Our Kitchen To Yours, 2009,
Debra's Natural Gourmet

The Little Shop That Could

Debra Stark / Publisher
Cover, book design and production by David Stark

Debra's Natural Gourmet
98 Commonwealth Ave.
Concord, MA 01742
978.371.7573
www.DebrasNaturalGourmet.com

ISBN 978-0-9742627-3-4

The Little Shop That Could

A retailer's love affair
with community and food

By Debra Stark

Debra's Natural Gourmet
Concord, Massachusetts

To Mom, who loved us.
May she forgive me for
spilling the beans.

Debra Stark

A man without a smiling face must not open a shop.

Chinese Proverb

"I never make a trip to the United States without visiting
a supermarket. To me, they are more fascinating than any
fashion salon."

Wallis Simpson, an American socialite later known as the Duchess of
Windsor, whose intended marriage to the British king, Edward VIII
led to his abdication.

"Eat food, less of it, mostly plants."

Michael Pollan, *In Defense of Food*

Acknowledgments

This book would never have seen the light of day were it not for all the characters who have entertained me these last thirty years. How could this book have come to be without Mr. Ogeltree or the story about dueling knives in the kitchen? As for the rest of you, you know who you are! I have been afraid to show you this book ahead of publication. In case I need to apologize for anything I said or should have said and didn't, mea culpa. I hope you enjoy the stories and won't set up picket lines in front of my house or the shop.

To Vivian Rush, my beloved accountant and friend who has finally retired but is still eager for updates on the going-ons and everyone in the shop, thanks for printing out the list of all the people who have worked at Debra's Natural Gourmet. Who knew there have been so many? Thanks for laughing with me at recollections of the bug man.

To my brothers, David and Daniel Stark, thanks for loving me. Thanks for the memories growing up with Mom and her egg drinks. Thanks, Daniel, for writing about Mom's bread and thanks, David, for sending me funny stories over the years. I saved them because I knew they would create the tone I wanted for the book I would one day write.

Another thanks, David, for turning my word document into a publishable book and for making creative suggestions. I owe the cover and my author's photo and new ending to you, Davey Crocket. I bet you didn't think I would remember that that's what Daniel and I called you when we were kids! (Daniel was Daniel Boone, and we three dressed up like frontiersmen and chased each other in the yard.)

Thanks to Adam, my son, for being with me in the store, for not saying "And what were you thinking!?!" anymore. Adam, this book wouldn't exist without your stories and emails which are, by turn, hilarious and serious. You are such a good writer and I hope someday you'll write your own book, and that's why I didn't include any of your articles.

To the companies in the natural products industry and Independent Natural Food Retailer's Association (INFRA) stores who appear in these pages, thank you, and may you always have delightful customers, just like we do.

To Kelly Notaras, founder of kn literary arts, whose workshop at Kripalu, and book, *The Book You Were Born to Write*, got me to sit and finally write this book. Thanks to Nikki Van De Car who helped me shape *The Little Shop* by advising me to combine some chapters, lose some material and then go forth and conquer, I couldn't have done it without you.

Table of Contents

Chapter One

Only At Debra's Natural Gourmet

It's the Saturday before Thanksgiving. It's just before five in the morning. Debra's Natural Gourmet is about to open doors to the noses pressed against the glass outside. It's dark out there. It's cold because it's November in New England. Some folks are sitting in their cars, drinking coffee to stay warm. Everyone is dressed in pajamas with coats thrown over. We see bunny slippers, boots and long wool scarves.

Inside, we have our pajamas on, too. We've gathered shopping carts, baskets, boxes with handles. We've brought an excess of nuts and honeys up from the basement to make sure we have plenty.

As we open the doors, there's a buzz. Folks who are our customers–neighbors, friends, workout buddies–rush in, bathrobes flapping, some with rollers in their hair. We see hunting caps, silly hats. We hand out warm muffins from our kitchen, there's free coffee and the music is jolly.

It's the start of the Early Bird Sale. All this friendly madness (it's tradition!) has been going on since the year after we opened.

Debra's Natural Gourmet, in historic Concord, Massachusetts, opened in October 1989. To be geographically accurate, our shop is located in West Concord, around the corner from the state prison. West Concord is not considered the classy side of town. We rarely see the tourists who flock to see the homes of Ralph Waldo Emerson, Louisa May Alcott, Nathaniel Hawthorne and Henry David Thoreau. But collectively, West Concord and Concord proper are known as the town where the shot fired was heard 'round the world. Concord, about twenty miles northwest of Boston, is where we Americans took on the British, and we're proud of it! Concord was also proud to be the first New England inland settlement. In 1681, the town meeting house had no heat, and so according to the *History of Concord, Massachusetts* by Rebecca Beatrice Brooks, "parishioners kept their feet warm with wolf skin bags that were attached to the pews or benches. They also brought dogs to church and rested their feet on or under the dog. Eventually dogs were prohibited in the church."

Isn't that a hoot?

During the American Revolution, Harvard University, located in Cambridge, Massachusetts, relocated classes to Concord because Boston was under siege. This makes perfect sense to me because one feels that Concord is a town where thinking and farming go hand in hand, where authors flourish and soil health matters. From then until today.

In that spirit, I decided to open a shop. There was an empty storefront, and the rents in West Concord were affordable.

I didn't have a clue about business, but having been brought up on organic food and natural medicine, I *knew* that if people would only eat real food, we'd all feel hunky-dory and health care costs in the good old USA would plummet.

My vision was a happy place where people would discuss politics, religion, food and health. Because Concord is a hotbed of genteel but lively discussions about all manner of topics that might be uncomfortable or even verboten elsewhere, I knew I'd chosen the perfect town. In our shop there would be no Styrofoam cups, nothing with white sugar, and the mood would be light. We'd have cowboy and classical music and be a little artsy (witness the carrot table at the front made by Billy Cosby and the huge carved wooden carrot hanging over the kitchen made by a former nun). We'd offer an eclectic mix of goods from around the world in addition to eggs, milk and lentils. I wanted a place that smelled good from pots of soup simmering on the stove and ginger cookies baking in the oven. I wanted people to swap recipes.

All I knew about the natural products industry was that, growing up, Mom, Beatrice Stark, ordered 50-pound bags of organic grains from California shipped to our home in Florida, which she ground to make her own breads. Mom loved garlic and used it with gay abandon. She cleaned with vinegar and water and tossed food scraps around the yard (this she called "broadcasting") to make her own compost.

This was plenty knowledge, I figured, to open a health food shop. After all, I rationalized, "How hard could it be?"

Paint walls, hire people, buy pots and pans, order peanut butter, extra virgin olive oil, purchase a cash register at Best Buy, turn on the lights, and voilà!

The day we opened we were shut down because we didn't have a license to sell dairy. Who knew that was a requirement?

On day two, the town closed us down again because we didn't have a Common Victualler's License. Today I pay more attention to what's needed, and we follow the rules. But my understanding of regulatory law is still fuzzy, and I'm lucky that I've got help in minding our p's and q's.

To stock the store, I had ordered 6,000 pounds of olives in five-gallon pails from California, convinced that everyone in Concord would love olives as much as I did.

It took eight years for us, the four members of the Stark family living in Concord (my parents, Sidney and Beatrice, and my son, Adam, and I) to eat those olives up. Yep, we also sold them in the shop, and because the olives were packed in brine or oil-cured, they didn't spoil. But still. That was a lot of olives.

And there were even more. I had also ordered a pallet of sixty cases of Graber Olives in cans, because Graber tree-ripened olives were a family favorite. Growing up, my brothers, David, Daniel, and I nicknamed Graber olives "butter olives." Taste one of these homely, tree-ripened olives, and you'll get it. It took a while to get folks to try them, but our shop still sells Graber olives, and they are a favorite today with customers who have adopted my enthusiasm. Graber olives are that good.

Back then, I met trucks coming up from Manhattan in the middle of the night driven by Russian immigrants who didn't speak English. They brought me smoked and pickled fish, which, like olives, I deemed a New England favorite. As with the olives, I was dead wrong. I was simply channeling Mom's Mom, Grandma Sarah, who loved pickled herring. She ate them every day with sharp, pungent white onion slices and black bread.

I had no clue that people in town were laughing, placing bets how long it would be before Debra's went under.

Of course, we had *some* customers. My modus operandi with these first, brave souls was to ask what they were looking for, and if we didn't have it (99 percent of the time), I'd write the item down in my spiral notebook, take their name and telephone number and tell them we'd have it in a day or two. I'd order from a distributor, whose trucks would deliver the next day. All monies that came in went out to buy inventory that people wanted, rather than inventory I thought they should want. This concept I got quickly.

Pricing was another matter altogether. Everything we bought came with a "suggested retail price" (SRP). I declared the SRP a scam, outrageous. "How could a cup of coffee cost $1.00?" I'd exclaim. And I priced my stock my way.

Thus, for six months, we lost money with every sale. I hadn't factored in expenses like rent. I thought God would fly down from the sky and make payroll and pay the water bill.

Today I understand that you multiply the price you pay for every item by a certain amount and that allows you to pay for potatoes, snow plowing and toilet paper. As for profit, that was only a glimmer in the joker's eye.

In the beginning, I cooked alone in our kitchen, which meant getting there in the wee hours to have food ready by the time the store opened at 8:30 a.m. When I got home at the end of long days, my son Adam would ask, "So what do we have to eat today that no one else would buy?"

I vacuumed and washed the floors each evening. That wasn't so hard because the store was smaller and didn't get the kind of foot traffic or the amount of deliveries we do today.

Despite all the mistakes I made, it never occurred to me that our shop could fail. I always felt that we had the goodwill of the town despite their initial mistrust of an interloper who had to ask where the voting polls were.

In 2019, 30 years later, the store is 3,200 square feet, plus our basement which serves as our office, break room, houses our walk-in refrigerators and freezers, and is a repository for window decorations and other paraphernalia. Even with all that space we're too crowded. We keep looking for more room so we can create wider aisles, give our kitchen the space they desperately need, and expand to do some fun things we dream of.

Today folks from the neighborhood swing in for a head of lettuce or kombucha on tap. Others come from all over New England. We get guests from around the world. Some come for ingredients they can't find elsewhere, and all our shoppers come for our staff.

We have 57 people on staff, and they range in age from 14 to 84. I'm proud that we respect and enjoy each other's differences. Mary Jane always wears her button that talks about freedom and diversity. We work with the prison work-release program. Rakhi brings us nibbles that remind her of her roots in India, and Pat is on a mission to connect everyone! Together, we've created a shop that is a haven in these modern times.

Debra's Natural Gourmet has been featured on *20/20*, in *Yankee Magazine*, the *NYT*, the *Boston Globe*, *Natural Food Merchandiser*, *Whole Foods Magazine*, our own local newspaper, *The Concord Journal*, and more. It's made our customers proud, but honestly they are a big reason for our success! Our shop's mission statement is "Community Through Food," and, yes, we borrowed this mission statement from a wonderful independent natural product store in San Francisco, called Bi-Rite.

Today Adam is co-owner. He and our next-gen staff (you'll meet them later) are putting their stamp on the business. They bring energy and passion. They want our shop to live on.

This book is about our staff, our customers, our industry. This book is the story of our shop, how it came to be and about the thirty years it's been a place we all call home. You'll share what we've learned on the journey. You'll share our discussions about food, health, organic, local, fair trade, biodynamic and how to change the world to make it more resilient and kinder. You'll find some favorite recipes and articles from our newsletters, because they're too good not to share. You'll find a chapter about our industry and sister stores around the country, my take on plastic cutting boards, potlucks, and get the scoop on surprising things we've learned in order to stay in business. You'll get to know us.

I've always loved what Adam wrote in 2006. It sums up who we are in a nutshell.

The day we bought our space

The day we finally bought our space on Commonwealth Avenue in West Concord and became masters of our own destiny, it occurred to me: we have 68 different kinds of lip balm.

The day before, when everything was still up in the air, it occurred to me: *this place feels like home.* On that day, a customer came up to me and told me that the store was an "anchor" in her life, a safe place, a constant. She could always count on us to be there. And by that, I gather, she didn't just mean be *in a place*, but to *be there*, for her, in ways that were unnameable.

I told her I felt the same way.

But I couldn't tell her about the building, the fact that it was on the open market and we might not get it, might be homeless in less than a month when our lease was up, might not *be there* anymore. Another buyer had just offered more than we thought we could afford. And the owners had promised to decide in two days.

We didn't have a Plan B. And frankly, I was scared.

Now, we have the space. And an enormous mortgage. And 68 different flavors of lip balm. These 68 flavors (and this number is constantly fluctuating) say something important about Debra's Natural Gourmet. It isn't very efficient. It doesn't reflect a Master Plan. I doubt they teach 68 flavors at business school.

These 68 flavors, added one at a time, reflect the community, what Wendell Berry calls a *membership*, that is the store, both its staff and its customers, extending outwards to its vendors, and its vendors' suppliers, and finally, to the farmers who bring food from the Earth. We stock Skye Botanicals lip balm, because Martha decided, independent of anyone, that it was too good not to have. Also, she knows Monica Skye, knows that Monica wildcrafts her own herbs. We stock Burt's Bees beeswax lip balm because Barbara says the peppermint oil in it makes her lips "tingly." We stock Mode de Vie Karité-Lips because of Debra. She likes that it contains Shea butter, which is closest of all butters to the oils found in our own skin. We stock Carlson vitamin E lip balm because John and Susan Carlson have been in business for all the right reasons since 1967. Now their children and grandchildren are part of the company. We stock The Merry Hempsters vegan lip balm because years ago a customer told Jim she loved it, couldn't live without it. We stock Galen's Way Lip Salve-ation because my ex-girlfriend knew the man who made them, and always said he was a great guy. He works out of a tiny herb shop in Maryland. And then just last month I noticed his name tucked into the corner of a catalog. It's his first product in distribution. And I figured, it looks good, why not give him some business?

Every one of those lip balms is there because of someone's enthusiasm, someone's commitment to an ideal. There is a story behind every one of our lip balms. And no one person knows them all. And that, I believe, is the point.

Chapter Two

Community, Putting Our Noses Against Each Other's Flanks

I look at horses relaxing in a field, touching noses affectionately, gently poking each other, and I realize that at heart, we, too, are herd animals. We need each other for warmth and comfort.

Some years back, in an article entitled, "It's Lonely Out There," Scott Allen of the *Boston Globe* wrote that we don't have as many close friends as we used to. We're socially isolated despite emails, text messaging, blogging and cell phones. There are fewer dinner parties, lower voter turnout, and falling participation in bowling leagues. We're reluctant to call a neighbor if we're in trouble.

Can you imagine that? Afraid to call a neighbor?

Allen noted, "This increasing social isolation started in 1965 with the rise of television, two-career households and the destruction of close-knit neighborhoods. Simply put, intimacy and community are getting lost in the rapid changes of American society."

It's no secret that social isolation contributes to depression and deteriorating physical health. Loneliness is said to be as much of a health risk factor as smoking. And, Allen wrote, only 4.9 percent of us have six close friends.

Personally, I have more than six close friends just amongst our staff, not to mention customers who enrich my life. That's why, on most days, we who work at Debra's love our job. That's why our crowded, beat-up little store with heart and soul is still in business.

It's all about kinship.

When people come in, they share "the good, the bad and the ugly." They share family difficulties, worries, that a broken bone healed fast, illness and the story about the dog eating the sausages left sitting on the counter. In addition to runners who finish the Boston Marathon and authors who have bestsellers, musicians who perform to great acclaim in London and artists who are in residence in exotic cities, we schmooze with our own doctors, plumbers, painters and next-door neighbors. We know Sadie is getting married and that Howie got a scholarship. We see photos of home gardens and hear stories about bunny rabbits eating pea plants, and gosh darn it, tomatoes right off the vine. We get invited to come pick blueberries.

Debra's Natural Gourmet is an antidote to isolation. Lou tells us she loves us. Barry relishes our newsletter which speaks to him "just like a letter from my best friend." Samantha says she comes in because we're a safe haven. Cindy, who used to work in the store, knows I appreciate a good joke. We get to see photos (on cell phones, nowadays) of grandchildren, kitties and scenery. Maxine comes in so she can poke in our personal shopping baskets and ask why we're buying what we're buying! She knows she can be a nosy parker and that she's still welcome.

There's a cheeriness in the air.

In the early years, before the renaissance in West Concord, we'd invariably get people right off the train on their way to visit someone at the prison, coming in and asking for a pack of cigarettes. They didn't know us. They were often incensed we didn't sell, on top of no cigarettes, frosty Coca-Cola.

Though smokes and Cokes aren't our style, they sure would have made paying the rent easier in the early days. Times were tough. People in town didn't embrace us with open arms, and we weren't an overnight success. We weren't a community, not yet.

To the old timers who remember our space as one that had housed a men's bar, then a red and white convenience store, and then a fish market, there was no place in town for a newfangled health food store. We weren't their tribe.

But we were lucky that there was already an organic farm in town, Hutchins Farm. We were lucky that there was a health food store called the Spice and Grain (aka "Spit and Grit") in another part of Concord, across Route Two. That meant there were at least two people who knew what we were about, and it was my hope they would wander in soon.

I was determined that our shop would become a gathering place. Neighbors would meet neighbors near the bean bins. We'd have the kind of customers who would buy homemade chicken soup to bring to Grandma. Who would want beeswax candles, and rose water to flavor an exotic recipe.

It was important to me to create community through food, to bring back the tradition of sitting around a table. "Pass the potatoes, please!" I wanted people to be comfortable in their own kitchens. I was (and am) hot to trot on sharing simple food and great conversation.

Today, with all the allergies and crazy schedules, sitting down together is a little more complicated. But I know, because people tell me, that neighborliness has rippled outward. People are dishing out soup to nourish family and friends, and sitting around tables and talking.

Together, our staff, customers and vendors make our community. While that community may not go up on the roof to shovel snow or help Jim Leahy (our store manager) hose down the air-conditioners in the summer heat, they witness our equipment breaking down. They've seen us rush to help when someone slips outside. David Abbott has driven more than one person to the hospital. We're there when someone locks themselves out of their cars or loses a wallet. We found Alice's bank card. We're there when Amy (not her real name) has a panic attack. When Bob's shingles make him double over in pain. Because we've become a meeting place, when the planes crashed into the towers in New York City on 9/11, and when the Boston Marathon bombing happened, people came into the shop for solace.

I still remember the time Carl (not his real name) refused a basket, his arms full of glass bottles. "Don't worry," he said. "I know how to juggle." He then dropped a bottle of cod liver oil that broke. The oil ran faster than we could to get rags to sop it up. It ran under metal shelving for miles, and there are days when I still imagine I smell cod liver oil.

You have to laugh when someone's toddler suddenly decides to go to the bathroom on the floor near the register. And then there is that stage when toddlers delight in taking off their clothes and running around naked.

Interesting times at Debra's!

To grow our community, we spoke to men's clubs, women's groups, colleges, schools, organizations like Emerson Hospital and The Rotary Club. I remember a talk on sustainability I gave at Concord Carlise High School years ago, where our kitchen also made and donated a meal for 200. The master of ceremonies genuinely and profusely thanked Whole Foods. Oh, well.

Like businesses in all the hometowns in the country, we give money to school fundraisers, donate to The Walk for Hunger, contribute to nonprofits who work on environmental issues, social justice issues, parenting, food politics, farming and climate action campaigns. We help with scholarship funds, as well as special funds we've set up for some of our customers who wouldn't be able to buy what they need otherwise.

We're supporters of organizations like Gaining Ground and Open Table. Today we donate to Dignity in Asylum and watchdog groups like Women's Voices From The Earth and Find the Cause Breast Cancer and the Organic Consumers Association. We have participated in Stone Soup, a dinner to celebrate local agriculture. With some of our neighbors, we founded Give Back Day in West Concord. In the last 30 years, our little shop has donated a million dollars to fight hunger and much more.

All these organizations are part of our community. But today, in this climate of isolation, people ask for donations over email or with a form letter. I miss the good old days when people would ask for raffle items when they came in to shop. There's nothing warm and fuzzy about receiving a letter that says, "Dear Merchant."

If you've been in our store you know our music creates harmony. It's funky. Our peeps hum along. Sometimes they whistle in the aisles. I've seen a two-step and a twirl.

What kind of music? Cowboy, "The Yellow Submarine," "Dipsy Doodle," Glenn Miller, "Do the Twist," along with classical and my fave protest songs from the sixties like "Blowin' in the Wind" and the Chad Mitchell Trio's "John Birch Society." Never dull, our music brings back memories. Young ones ask, "What the heck?" when they hear Eddie Cantor sing, "Yes Sir, That's My Baby."

"How Much is That Doggie in the Window," however, drove our staff bonkers, and after 20 years on shuffle, random, repeat, I think it's finally been deleted. I kind of liked it. Arrf, arrf.

I heard Adam telling a customer one day that he found himself humming a song he'd despised for years (it wasn't "hip enough") but now he kinda liked it. I wager that someday the teenagers who go on from our store will hum "The Marvelous Toy" and "Ma, He's Making Eyes at Me" to their children and grandchildren!

That's a coming together, isn't it?

It's given me such pleasure to put in a Chanukah window each year with my menorah collection. When I was growing up, there were only Christmas windows, and I felt excluded. So today, we have both Christmas and Chanukah, and sometimes we celebrate Buddha's birthday and Chinese New Year, too.

Recently, someone asked me if, in today's political climate, I wasn't afraid to put in a Chanukah window again. It hadn't occurred to me to be afraid, because I so enjoy all the people who live around me. It hadn't occurred to me that some might not enjoy me right back.

People are fond of us, and in this age of sexual harassment and people who behave badly, we offer heartfelt hugs. We had a customer set up a table outside the store on Valentine's Day giving out free hugs.

Over the years we've had families ask if they could hold hands and remember a loved one in our store, because Debra's meant so much to their father, their sister, their grandmother.

Our annual October Food Fair is great fun. It was first founded to celebrate the shop's birthday and call attention to Non-GMO month, but then morphed into Discover West Concord Day, with all our neighbors throwing a party, too. It's a big bash, and in our store, it gives our customers a taste of what it feels like to be at a natural products show. They can experience walking the floor, tasting, meeting the folks who are responsible for Bob's Red Mill and Nettle Meadows cheeses. If you've never tasted smoked olive oil, we want to give you a chance. And avocado ice cream, too.

We fit in about 40 vendors. Some are local and some come from half the way around the world. They set up tables outside on the sidewalk and throughout our 3,200 square foot store. "Prepare to feel like a sardine!" we tell everyone. It's that crowded. Produce tables get moved outside into the alley between our shop and the 5&10 next door to make more room. Our kitchen bakes cupcakes served with ice cream (yep, we have gluten-free and dairy-free options) and we dish out recipes like polenta with beans and greens and lots of cheese. If we don't make this cheesy polenta, we get "What the heck?!?" from our customers. They love this dish. They demand it.

One-Skillet Polenta with Black Beans, Greens and Cheese

Yes, this is a rustic, peasant-style dish which provides lots of energy! Yes, it's a snap to make when you use ready-made polenta. And it's lovely that there's only one pot to wash. There are variations on this theme too. In my first cooking class with kids, we put portabella mushroom caps in the skillet instead of polenta and sliced zucchini instead of leafy greens.

This dish makes it easy to get more beans in your diet. Beans have been an important part of the human diet for thousands of years because they are satisfying, healthy and good for the planet! Black turtle beans are a great source of protein and cholesterol-lowering fiber, which also prevents blood sugar levels from rising too rapidly after a meal, making these beans an especially good choice for individuals with diabetes, insulin resistance, hypoglycemia or anyone trying to lose weight. And the USDA says black beans are one of the top ten antioxidants right up there with blueberries.

Serves 4-6

4 Tbsp extra virgin olive oil	24 oz pasta sauce (like Les Moulins
1 pk Food Merchant organic polenta	Mahjoub or Primal Kitchen)
1 can (15 oz) Eden black beans	16 oz grated melting cheese
4 Tbsp grated Pecorino Romano	(it's easier if you use cheese slices) *
1 lb greens like kale, spinach,	1 tsp each oregano, basil, thyme
chard, broccoli	

Drizzle olive oil in a large skillet. Open roll of polenta and cut into half-inch slices. Cover bottom of skillet with slices. Open can of Eden beans with all that terrific taste and fiber...Eden cooks its beans with a piece of kombu (kelp, which is seaweed) so they're easy to digest. Drain them. Spoon beans evenly over polenta. Sprinkle with Romano. Rinse and shake greens. Chop coarsely into bite-sized pieces and spread in skillet. Cover with pasta sauce, then cheese. Sprinkle with dried herbs (they make the dish look prettier when you go to serve it). Put lid on skillet and simmer 5 minutes. Serve to cries of delight, with a tossed salad or sliced cucumbers and cut up tomatoes. You've served up protein, fiber and great carbs. This dish is truly energy food.

Feel free to bake this dish in the oven instead of cooking on the stove top. 350 degrees, covered, for 30 minutes ought to do it. If you can't do dairy, do non-dairy cheese that will be "melty" on top. You could also use shrimp, if you like that kind of combination.

*My favorite melting cheese used to be Applegate Farms sliced Havarti. This cheese went away when Hormel Foods acquired Applegate in 2015.

• •

George comes from Greece, and graces us with his tall Zorba-the-Greek appearance, sampling Spartan olive oil, and the folks from Mount Mansfield Maple, located in Vermont, offer samples of Oprah Winfrey's favorite syrups and maple candies. Belal flew from afar last year with coconut sugar and Himalayan pink salt. We sample Cappello's gluten-free pastas and Tucson Tamales that are to die for. We've had John Paino, who lives in Concord, sample his #9 chips and salsa, and the swoffles that he and his daughter Julia perfected. Swoffles, otherwise known as stroopwafel or Dutch waffles, are delish! Walden Meats grills sausages, and Hodo Soy samples spicy yuba noodles.

One year, the Canadian consulate sent representatives because we had two Canadian companies, including Jelinas, which makes fabulous chocolates (my fave being one with maple sugar crystals), and Koukla Delights ("Koukla" means "little darling" in Armenian) that makes an organic raw coconut macaroon with flavors like matcha, vanilla and chocolate.

Elizabeth comes with Dancing Moon mushrooms she grows locally. Shelburne Farms comes from Vermont to sample their cheddars, and we serve teas like Mem and Rishi and coffees and kombuchas. Nut butters and Miyoko vegan butter are adored. Real grass-fed cow butters like Ploughgate get slathered on Manna sprouted seed bread. Our customers get to sample dishes with coconut oil, ghee and black garlic, and meet Victoria who comes with her artisanal, small batch halvah ("Halvah Heaven"), now gone national.

The lineup changes each year.

But honestly, we try to find interesting products year-round, not just at our Food Fair. We're willing to go out on a limb and bring in items that are truly original, even when they seem to cost an arm and a leg. We want these companies in our wheelhouse. We want them to be part of our community.

To give you an example of one such company that is now part of our wheelhouse, Adam learned about Vermatzah through Guido's, a sister independent natural products retailer. Vermatzah makes their matzah by hand from ancient grains grown in Vermont. "Vermatzah offers foodies and locavores interested in healthy eating and sustainable agriculture a tasty alternative!" Vermatzah says. "We then infuse the 5,000-year-old tradition of baking matzah by the open fire in small, handmade batches ensuring the freshest quality."

Vermatzah has been a success for us, but we don't always make the right call. Not all companies become part of the neighborhood. We went out on a limb and fell off hard when we brought in Desert Camel's camels' milk in 2014. Desert Camel has small family farms around the US, and their smallest family farm in Ohio has only two camels. They say, "Now that's what we call cozy."

(No, I don't know how a camel is milked but I can imagine. I do know I wouldn't want to be the milker).

I took a chance on Desert Camel because I read that autistic children and diabetics who drank camel's milk derived great benefit. I was the butt of laughter from our staff, until folks started coming to our shop from great distances to buy it. We were the only store on the east coast carrying camels' milk at that time, and parents who drove from neighboring states swore their kids got more help from camels' milk than from medication. But we had to stop carrying it when it became easier and less expensive for our customers to purchase it online (16 oz costs $18 online today).

Our local suppliers create the strongest sense of community. Folks want to be part of their neighbor's success. Folks want to feel that because of their support, their rah-rah-ing, those vegan magic muffins made it to Shark Tank or to Oprah or Dr. Oz.

We've had many a discussion about whether it's more important to buy an organic apple that had to be transported across country, or an apple grown in town, but with chemical fertilizers and pesticides. Is organic garlic shipped from California, for instance, good for the consumer but bad for the food system? Do those of us who live in New England even have a choice when there's snow on the ground?

The best of both worlds is when we find a local, organic farm like Old Frog Pond Farm in Harvard, MA.

Harvard-up-the-road is clearly local, but how do we define what local is in other cases? Whole Foods' John Mackey uses a radius of 200 miles to define local. For us that means much of New England and some parts of New York State.

Advocates of local eating who don't care so much about organic say that what happens after harvest–how food is shipped and handled–is more important than how it was grown. Locavores.com, a site popular among local purists, asserts that "because locally grown produce is freshest, it is more nutritionally complete." Does this outweigh the higher antioxidant content of organic or negate the use of pesticides and herbicides?

If I have my druthers, my tribe are the organic farmers and organic food producers. I opt for organic and keep Food for Life-brand sprouted whole-grain breads in my freezer from the west coast rather than Iggy's, who are local but use white flour. I won't buy Dancing Deer cookies because of regular old white-death sugar and white flour. That's how I was brought up, but I understand that not everyone who comes through our doors feels the same, and that's fine. It's good when our towns and neighborhoods and shops are not all vanilla ice cream, but toffee and orange creamsicle. It's good when we can have a respectful conversation.

Remember that Early Bird sale I mentioned? That first year, we had only one jim-cracky register from Best Buy, a $99 special. Taken by surprise, we were mobbed by people who acted as if a sale was a brand-new invention. People showed up in pajamas, boisterous with laughter. They chatted with neighbors and made new friends as they waited in lines that wound around our then tiny 1,200-foot store. No one seemed to mind waiting for over an hour to reach the register for 20 percent off. I kid you not. It was a blast. Nightcaps hobnobbed with sweats and quilted robes. There were some satin and lace outfits as well.

A few of us tried to check people out via hand-held Texas Instrument calculators (the cat's meow in those days). Standing in the aisle, one customer cheerfully forked over hundreds of dollars more than he should have–my fingers are not tiny, and those keypads are made for three-year-olds. Around dinner time, he came back, and we were able to make things right. John is still a customer in the store today.

One year, a woman arrived at the Early Bird sale accompanied by police. She'd driven to the store in a negligee covered by a raincoat. But she stopped at the public library on her way because she wanted to kill two birds with one stone and return her books by putting them in the book drop. The police didn't believe her story about an early morning sale where people came in sleeping attire until they witnessed Early Bird for themselves.

Lights outside our store are relatively new. So, the police arriving with our hapless customer in tow would have seen cars in the dark, more arriving, and people with their noses pressed against the glass waiting for us to ring the opening bell so the mad dash into the shop could begin.

You can always tell that people are having a gay old time. Conversations with perfect strangers waiting side by side in lines are often hysterically funny. And shopping is contagious–Rhonda might mention how much she loved a particular honey or maple syrup, and people in line around her would ask John or Jane Doe to save their place as they dashed to swarm the honey and maple syrup aisles, returning triumphant with a new favorite item for their cupboards.

This is still true today. The rule is that if you are in the door by the end of the Early Bird, 9:00 a.m., you can stay as long as you like and still get the twenty percent Early Bird discount. There were years you'd see people still shopping at noon wearing pjs or bathrobes alongside people who were regular Saturday shoppers. The regulars who'd arrived after the melee would wonder what the heck was going on.

One year, when we still had to key in each item's price, digit by digit, and long before we had scanning registers, a customer who arrived about 7:00 a.m., was still there at two in the afternoon. She'd filled shopping cart after cart when carts were needed by many. When she was finally finished, it took three of us an hour and a half to ring her up. She had spent thousands. As we wheeled everything out to the back parking lot and her car, we realized before she did and with some consternation that her purchases would not fit into her car. She called her husband who came down with his pickup truck. We slunk away as the two of them got into a heated discussion. It was our hope he would see the humor in the situation and have the good grace to laugh. After all, she got all her Christmas shopping done.

Today, every mall has Early Bird sales. And registers have scanners that beep. In our store, Early Bird is now streamlined, with people easily heading home in time for pancakes and coffee.

It isn't the same community event it once was. Yet customers still look forward to it each year and thank us for giving them the chance to start their holiday shopping at a discount.

I keep trying to figure out what's next that still has an old-fashioned community feel now that registers beep. I want something that slows us down and gives us a chance to mingle more. At the end of the day, I think, we are still herd animals, and we need to be able to put our noses into the flanks of others for warmth and comfort. Debra's is that kind of place.

Chapter 3

Mom, Family, And Growing Up

I never would have opened Debra's Natural Gourmet were it not for Mom.

Picture a cocktail party. Beatrice Stark, my progressive, politically active, book-reading and delightful mother, charmed the socks off whomever she met. She navigated tricky conversational topics with grace. She was not a cocktail party kind of person. She was much more comfortable in the garden or biking with a friend. Nonetheless, she would have bested Dr. Frederick Stare, chairman of the Department of Nutrition at Harvard's School of Public Health, who declared no difference between white bread and whole grain. She would have gazed at him as he stated we are the best-fed people in the world, that organic food was no better than food grown with chemical fertilizers. She would have asked, "Oh, do you really think so?"

Her method was to ask a question. To give people breathing room, the chance to think. In Dr. Stare's case, she would have let him hoist himself on his own petard. She was too much of a lady to have brought up the fact that he procured massive amounts of funding for Harvard and his own research over the years from food-manufacturing giants such as Coca-Cola, General Foods, and the National Soft Drinks Association.

She might have quoted Margaret Mead, who said, "It is easier to change a man's religion than to change his diet." Yes, I was brought up on organic food and natural medicine. I've never known anything but. No pesticides, no herbicides, no white sugar, no white flour. That was the mantra in the Stark household.

Mom used to say that if people used their noggins, they'd realize that refined foods are stripped of many nutrients. She was a great one for commonsense. Why, she'd ask, did we go along with Madison Avenue's line that, in the case of wheat, it's better when the healthy bran and nutrient-dense germ are removed? Bran and germ are removed because, if they're not super fresh, they turn rancid. Which means that when they are taken away, the "improved" flour or bread or baked goods can sit on the shelf for many moons. "And this benefits whom?" she would ask.

All this made me who I am today and is why I opened the shop.

Wheat germ and brewer's yeast (nutritional yeast today) were superfoods. You ate them and could leap tall buildings. You ate them and they not only cleaned your room and did your homework but turned you into an honor student.

The three of us (my brothers David, Daniel and I) were shooed outside to eat rose hips off the 100 bushes of *rosa rugosa* (wild rose) Mom had persuaded Pop (Sid Stark) to plant. Rose hips are a rich source of vitamin C, she would tell us. "You don't want to catch Rickey's cold," she would say.

Her health heroes were actress Gloria Swanson and her own sister, our Aunt Anna. Aunt Anna wasn't famous and had no fortune, but she and Gloria were both opinionated. Both were bona fide health nuts. That's what the public called people who watched what they ate.

It was Gloria Swanson who said, "I thought I had ulcers because if you are a producer, you are supposed to have ulcers." Her doctor asked what she'd eaten the night before. Then he asked her to "mentally picture putting all this food in a pail and then tell me what animal, including a pig, would eat it?" After this, Gloria said, "I was in a business of make-believe to entertain people, but I'll be darned if I want to eat make-believe food!"

As David, Daniel and I sat on the front stoop eating a whole watermelon each for dinner, the juice running down our arms (it was August, and we were dressed in swim suits), Mom told us Gloria was on an airplane eating an organic mango and avocado wearing white gloves.

Gloria was a tough act to follow. But Aunt Anna and Mom did their utmost, and their mother, our Grandma, Sarah Lefer, had set an example by using hard-earned pennies to feed her family real food. Hippocrates, after all, had declared "Let food be thy medicine!" Then he drank hemlock, as the courts of his time decreed.

Aunt Anna used to claim that people were in denial about sugar, cornstarch and MSG. She was always on her soapbox. She annoyed the heck out of most everyone. We were lucky that our mom believed in live and let live, except when it came to her own children. But in public, she didn't proselytize.

I hope I'm more my mother and not Aunt Anna in the store.

As a child, at the birthday party of a classmate, one of the moms brought me cake and ice cream. Hands behind my back, I said, so I've been told, "My mother doesn't let me eat that no good rotten stuff!"

When it was my turn to parent, I turned into my mother (without her charm). Just ask my son, Adam, about the "hot stuff" I concocted with honey, cayenne pepper, prepared horseradish and sometimes apple cider vinegar, for anytime we had sore throats or were getting sick. He threatened to report me to the authorities because torture, he claimed, was not an acceptable means of childrearing.

Am I a crackpot? I hope not. When Adam broke a leg, we went to the doctor. When I had a stroke, Adam took me to the hospital. (I tell people that I never get sick, which is almost true. Rarely do I get a cold. The flu? Never. But I did have a stroke. I named said stroke after a former husband because of the extreme stress he caused.)

I am, for sure, a health nut. I've been called worse. I grew up in Orlando, Florida, and I was called all kinds of names because it was the South and I was told I was a damn Northerner–from California and Maryland.

When we went northwards from Florida to visit family, we always ate at Ratner's. Ratner's was a famous Jewish deli founded in 1905 (it closed in 2002). In its heyday, Ratner's served Sunday brunch to 1,200 people each week, and patrons included Al Jolson, Fanny Brice, Jackie Mason, Elia Kazan, Walter Matthau, Groucho Marx, Robert Kennedy, Nelson

Rockefeller…and even the occasional mafia member. My favorite dish from Ratner's? Their cold vegetable soup made with sour cream. This is my version from those childhood memories.

I have all these herbs growing in my garden. If you don't, of course you can use dried herbs, about a third the quantity called for. Can't do dairy? There are dairy alternatives that work just fine.

Yes, we made this on *Eat Well Be Happy*, our cooking show. The crew loved this soup. Do use organic or grass-fed dairy products. It's so important.

Almost-like-Ratner's Summer Soup

Serves 6

1 C plain kefir or yogurt*	½ C minced red onion
1 C sour cream	2 tsp good salt
½ C minced parsley	1 Tbsp fresh minced dill weed
1 clove garlic, pressed	1 tsp fresh oregano leaves
1 C diced cucumber (with skin)	1 Tbsp fresh basil
¼ C diced green scallions	Garnish: more sour cream, dill,
¼ C halved and sliced radishes	radishes, chives

Using a blender, food processor or Vitamix, quickly combine kefir, sour cream, parsley and garlic. Pour into a large bowl, add remaining ingredients, except garnishes. Refrigerate until very cold. Serve with whatever garnishes you choose (I use them all, especially more sour cream!)

Got chronic bronchial flare-ups, sinus infections or asthma? Try radishes because they decongest, and they are said to prevent and shorten the duration of UTIs. Don't know the difference between yogurt and kefir? It's the kind of bugs (bacteria) present. Yogurt is the beer of probiotic dairy foods, while kefir is said to be the champagne.

*Two kefirs I have in my home fridge now are the Green Valley, lactose-free plain kefir and Redwood Hill goat kefir. I love both. If you haven't tried them, please do and tell me what you think.

• •

I suppose I do stand apart from the Jiffy peanut butter crowd, and my brothers as well, though they adopted different tenets of Mom's beliefs. David refinished Mom's salad bowl with care. He uses her bowl because it reminds him of her and the huge salads she used to make. Daniel knows how to make Mom's beef stew and still knows to "start his engine" in the morning by drinking a large glass of water. However, he has been known to have jars of Cool-Whip in his fridge. Mom is spinning in her grave (where did that saying come from?), mea culpaing to Gloria and wondering where she went wrong.

But to this day, we three love kasha (buckwheat groats). We salivate when we remember kasha for breakfast with milk and raisins. We make kasha as an accompaniment to crispy, roast chicken.

Mom was a terrific cook, and her chocolate cakes were the stuff of dreams. Which is why her conversion to carob (carob does *not* taste like chocolate and we should never pretend otherwise) was so disheartening. To this day my brothers blame me, and I have no idea why!

The green grocers at the Orlando A&P and Piggly-Wiggly supermarkets believed Bea raised rabbits because there was no way, they insisted, a family of five could eat ten heads of romaine and other assorted lettuce varieties each week. Not to mention bunches of watercress and parsley, too.

Two heads of lettuce per salad was like science fiction to the fellows who stocked produce. This was the summer that the movie called "The Creeping Unknown" was popular, and the screen was filled with algae. These men worried about what was going on in our house.

When we three D's got home from school, we'd take turns washing and patting lettuce leaves dry with linen towels. There were no salad spinners in the olden days. Mom, if she had time, would do the washing for us. She'd put the greens into a large, homemade terry-cloth sack she made from old towels. Occasionally, if the weather was cool and breezy, she'd hang the bag on the clothes' line in the backyard.

We'll always remember the day the sack of washed greens was brought in, dumped into the salad bowl, and exploded with crickets, who had somehow gotten into the bag. Their excitement and desire to get away from us was a wonder to behold. Corralling them and putting them back outside was no easy feat, either. We ate out that night, and Mom never again hung bags of washed greens out to dry.

If we ate green salads five nights a week, that left one night to eat out and one night for a grated salad made of raw carrots, beets and apple, together with diced fresh pineapple, some mango juice, sometimes raisins, served with avocado slices and sprigs of parsley (as with all salads in the Stark household, this salad was merely the first course). The grated salad, Mom said, would enrich our blood, help keep blood pressure low and give us clear, clean skin.

My brothers and I still make Mom's grated salad, and it's one of the standard recipes in the kitchen at Debra's Natural Gourmet, as well! In our store, a child named it the "Glowing Salad." Make it and you'll understand why.

This recipe is one of six recipes from our first cookbook repeated in our third cookbook, *The Blue-Ribbon Edition, From Our Kitchen To Yours*. It's a winner and I don't want you to miss it.

Growing up, we scrubbed the carrots, beet and apple. Then we hand-grated them. Did anyone have food processor back then? I don't think so. Which meant that, invariably, knuckles got grated along with carrots, beet and apple.

Our recipe says, "Don't bother to peel these veggies because 1) who has time to peel, and 2) most of the vitamins are either in the skin, or just below it, so why waste nutrients!"

Glowing Salad

Serves 4

1 fresh pineapple, cubed	1 C mango juice
1-2 large carrots	1 C raisins, optional

1 apple, halved, core taken out	4 sprigs parsley
1 med red beet, trimmed and halved	1 Hass avocado

Peel and cut pineapple into bite-sized cubes. Put in mixing bowl. Scrub carrots, apple and beet. Trim but don't peel.

Using the coarse grating blade of a food processor, grate carrots, apple and beet. Add to pineapple in bowl together with the juice and raisins (if you are using them). Mix salad well so you don't have clumps of beet. The whole salad will be rosy. Chill, covered, in the refrigerator for about an hour before serving. Can be made the day before. Spoon onto romaine lettuce leaf and garnish with parsley and peeled sliced avocado.

Kids love this salad!

• •

There were nights Mom took a vacation from scratch cooking, and she'd line us up at the door. When Pop walked in from work, he'd laugh, and we'd march out the door to favorite restaurants.

At home we had to eat what was served ("This is not a restaurant!" our mother would tell us). Eating out was a treat, and we got to choose what we wanted. We were in charge of our own meal when we ate out, and we loved that.

Johnny Aquino's authentic pizza with scamorze, provolone and fresh mozzarella? Yes! At Freddy's Steak House, it was Caesar salad tossed at the table with garlicky croutons and anchovies. At Chez Aileen's it might be "the little steak without bones," and we'd all order Mousse

Au Chocolat. Aileen used local heavy cream from cows that peacefully munched on grass long before the term "grass-fed." She left chunks of French chocolate in her hand-folded mousse. You got the creamy richness with a bite of heaven. The sour pickles at Ronnie's delicatessen were the best.

When we went to Chinese restaurants, the refrain, however, had tinges of home. All waiters wrote down, "No sugar, no corn starch, no MSG." At least we think that's what they wrote down. None of us could read or write or speak Mandarin, so we really had no clue.

Mom entertained grudgingly. That's not to say she didn't enjoy people and make everyone feel welcome. But at heart, she wanted meals to be intimate, a time for family to sit together and talk about politics, religion and what happened at school. So when Colonel Chow came to this country and worked with Pop, he'd say, "Bea, invite 30 to 40 guests. I'll make dinner!" He'd give her a shopping list and would mess up the kitchen good but create a meal for an emperor. When he left the Defense Department, moved to San Francisco and opened a Chinese restaurant, Mom breathed a sigh of relief.

Our two refrigerators (we always had two) were filled with produce of all kinds, lots of nuts like cashews, glass jars of ancient grains, homemade peanut and almond butter, blue-cheese and goat cheeses and wonderful yellow cheeses from around the world. Flax, sunflower and pumpkin seeds. Unhulled sesame seeds and freshly ground cornmeal to make corn crisps.

In the cupboard there were beans like garbanzos and black beans, French blue lentils, sardines with bones in extra virgin olive oil, cans of Graber olives and Ventresca tuna. There were always several bottles of extra virgin olive oils from around the world opened and in use.

From a culinary perspective, we were outliers. We were different from the folks who ate Hostess Ding Dongs and Cheez Whiz processed cheese spread. When friends came over, their eyes bugged out. They'd never seen the foods we ate. I'd always reassure them that we ate exactly what they ate, just different versions. I'd show them my jar of Arrowhead Mills' Deaf Smith Country peanut butter, the first organic peanut butter, and the first to use the difficult-to-grow Valencia peanut. The ingredients were simply peanuts and maybe some salt.

But to make matters worse, Mom juiced for us every day. We came home from school to fresh, raw vegetable juice. I didn't appreciate this sacrifice of time on the part of our mother, and I hated the juice. Back then.

Pop, strangely enough, was agreeable to what he was served. He would tuck his daily baggie of pumpkin seeds in his briefcase without complaint. He would eat them because Mom wanted no prostate problems in our house.

I remember the 50-pound bags of organic grains Mom had shipped from across the country. In those days, we didn't worry about fuel or trucking costs, and in those days, California and the west coast was pretty much the only place you could get organically grown grains—or produce, for that matter.

An exception was Mr. Ogeltree. who had acres and acres of organic citrus of all kinds in Orlando, Florida, not far from our house. When I met him, his back was crooked and he was missing most of his teeth. He was retired and done. He wanted Mom to visit and fill bags with citrus. He would accept no more than $1 a bag, but he'd cackle and pinch Mom's bottom as she climbed the ladder. I was brought along as protection. "Mr. Ogeltree, the child! What would your wife think?" From experience, I can tell you that this approach didn't work.

Did I appreciate the juice and all this organic stuff? Nope. Today Bea's homemade bread would have a cult following. But back then, I couldn't imagine anyone getting giddy about it. In the 1950's, sitting in the waiting room at the orthodontist, dully holding a sandwich made with Mom's bread, the orthodontist came out to get me. He stared in fascination at my Mack truck-sized sandwich. He asked to taste a piece of our mother's bread.

I gave him a piece. He chewed. He chewed more (you had to chew a lot with Mom's bread). He turned to Mom and offered her $40 a loaf and asked for two loaves to be delivered the following week. Mom thought he was joking. The orthodontist (I wish I remembered his name) said he wasn't, and at that moment, my interest in food took a serious turn.

Daniel, on the other hand, feels that Mom's bread scarred him for life. In his book, *Silence of the Bunnies*, he wrote, "Bread should be flexible. Most is. My mother made her own… bread…and it did not bend. If you got it the first day or two after it was made, it crumbled into a million little pieces when you bit it. After the second day, I would remember wistfully when mere teeth could put a dent in the bread. It would become so hard that you could only hope to take a bite by putting your full weight and strength into the effort. Generally, this didn't work. When it did, the breakthrough would be so violent that the sandwich contents would end up exploding into the air for a respectable distance. This would never fail to impress the kids around you."

While Daniel ate his sandwich (at least I think he did), I often traded mine for Wonder Bread and margarine, which I thought divine. When I wasn't able to do that, my lunch would fertilize the woodlands.

We had to eat all our lunch. That was Mom's decree. But she packed three or four courses, like pineapple cut into pieces and packed in an old glass jar, all of which took a lot of time chewing. And the school allotted 25 minutes for lunch, including time out for horsing around and talking to friends.

My cut apples were what mostly got flung into the woods, until the day our mother took a walk and found an apple half. Hers were easily distinguishable by the core neatly cut out. By the time she found it, the apple was moldy, but she brought it home and waited for me. I don't remember what she said, and I'm sure it had something to do with children starving in another part of the world. But I do remember that she made me take a bite to impress upon me that "We do not waste food!"

Thereafter, we compromised. Mom packed less food, and I chewed faster.

Today I make Mom's bread, though I've simplified it greatly using an organic seven-grain cereal instead of measuring out a dozen or so individual ingredients. As long as my seven-grain cereal has millet, I'm golden. And I shape my dough, not into loaves, but into pancake-shaped disks so the bread is easy to eat and there's no cutting slices involved.

The store stopped making Mom's Bread because our kitchen is just too small, overloaded, and because our Change-Your-Life Crisps eclipsed Mom's Bread in popularity. I hope, one day, when we've been able to expand, we'll go back to baking it. If for no other reason than the hilarious memories.

Mom's Bread – Made Much Easier

Made much easier because I've also dispensed with yeast. I figure that flatbreads don't need to rise. These are a meal unto themselves served with nut butter, butter, cheese, jam or honey, or nibbled plain. Great for breakfast.

Makes 28 flat breads — Bake at 350 degrees

2 C einkorn or whole wheat	1 Tbsp sea salt (like Celtic)
bread flour*	1 C flax seeds
4 C wholegrain 7-grain cereal	1 C pumpkin seeds, coarse chopped
¼ C bran (any) or chia seeds	1 C whole brown sesame seeds
2 C rolled oats	2 Tbsp caraway seeds
2 Tbsp molasses or honey, opt.	6+ C warm water

In a large bowl, mix all the ingredients together (use only 6 C water at this point). If batter seems dry after letting it sit for 20 minutes add another couple of cups of water. You'll get the hang of this over time, and it's nothing to worry your pretty little head about. A little less water, a little more, it's all good. You just want the dough to hold together. The last time I made these I used 8 C water. Go figure.

Preheat oven to 350 degrees.

Grease baking sheets. Place ⅓ C dough per bread disk onto baking sheet about 3 inches apart. Flatten each slightly with the palm of the hand (wetting hands makes this easier).

Put baking sheets in oven. Bake bread about 30 minutes, or until disks are lightly browned and you can scoot them around the baking sheet with your fingers (in other words, the batter is released from the pan).

If you like your bread crunchy, bake a little longer or pat them out thinner.

*Last time I made these I decided to use pumpkinseed flour instead of most of the einkorn or bread flour. My son Adam said he thought they were the best I'd ever made. See! Feel free to play with the recipe.

Note: Make a batch and freeze most. You can also bake until your breads have no more moisture and they're like hardtack. They travel great, and you have survival food.

• •

Another example of our mom's health nuttiness was her smoothies. It was hard to believe that this was the same firebrand who paraded with placards that said, "Elect so-and-so," and who elegantly attended Martin Marietta dinners (I still have a bag hanging behind my closet door with her gold slingback shoes I so loved). It was hard to believe that this was the same woman who introduced us to great literature and took us to plays and concerts.

Long before smoothies were popular, our mother made them, but she called hers "the egg drink." Brudder Daniel called them the "dreaded egg drink" in his book, and he wrote that Mom made it thick enough so a spoon would stand up. Egg drinks were her vehicle to keep Pop, who worked many hours, traveled a lot and lived a stressful life, as healthy as she could while letting him get out the door quickly. Extra special ingredients I remember were lecithin, rice bran, wheat germ oil, frozen bananas, carob powder and bone meal.

Whereas Pop had a cast iron stomach and would eat or drink just about anything that was pureed, our brother David suffered mightily. He'd drink like the good kid he was, and then throw up. His morning routine on the days Mom made her egg drink was drink, go throw up, run to catch the school bus.

Daniel wrote, "It was made with a raw egg base, into which would be poured all sorts of healthy powders —dolomite, carob, calcium or frankly anything that had received a favorable write-up in *Prevention Magazine*. This was then mixed together in a blender with water, or milk if the latter was starting to go bad. It produced a brown-looking drink, with a brackish head of foam. It chilled the soul to look at it… but Mom was always looking to improve it. In fact, our liberation from egg drinks came the day she decided to add the eggshells along with the eggs, in order to increase the calcium content. Why not? It would all go through the blender. The usual decibel level at the breakfast table went off the charts, and my mother finally agreed to taste her own drink to see what all the fuss was about. She immediately pronounced it undrinkable and asked in complete and maddening sincerity why we had never said something about it."

If she'd had a Vitamix, she might have gotten away with the eggshells. (Shades of Mom: Today Adam adds all manner of healthy ingredients into smoothies he makes for Mira, his toddler, my granddaughter. She loves them, he says. That's his story, at any rate.)

Pop, however, never complained about the egg drink, and she continued to make them for him most mornings until he retired from Raytheon and they lived in Concord, MA. She perfected them, and she (and Pop) said they were delicious. A little cinnamon and vanilla did wonders to make them taste just like a chocolate milkshake, she would say, still using carob.

Luckily for all of us, the breakfast menu varied, and we all loved oatmeal with mix-ins, homemade pancakes with fresh strawberries on top, leftover hamburger with melted cheddar and a grated carrot salad.

Her whole life, Mom repeated that she was counting on God to let her know when she had six months to live so could put on a mu'umu'u and eat nothing but pizza and ice cream. Though she quoted Erma Bombeck who said, "Seize the moment. Remember all those women on the Titanic who waved off the dessert cart," she still determined she would wait until her last six months before indulging. But at the end, what she craved was steamed broccoli, and because it tasted sweet, she accused me of melting sugar on it. She never did put on a mu'umu'u or eat the ice cream I bought for her.

Mom informed the person I am today. If I'd had a different mother, I'd probably be buying frozen tee-vee dinners. If it weren't for Mom, there would have never been a Debra's Natural Gourmet.

Chapter 4

Early Days Of The Store With Bea

My timing was not impeccable. In the recession of 1989, I opened Debra's Natural Gourmet with financial help from my parents and my brothers. Mom was in her glory. The shop was a place where she could help people, and a place where she could say to all comers, "Did my daughter order those rotten plums?" Pop, on the other hand, almost never came into the store. I'd spot him on the sidewalk across the street going into Phillips Hardware, not looking over, not seeing me waving like crazy. He never thought our shop would last. In fact, years later he said that both the store and I turned out "rather better than I expected." That was Pop. He was exasperating, but we three loved him anyway.

Memories of Mom are everywhere in the store. Folks still come in and tell me they remember her teaching them how to bake yams. She shared home remedies. Apple cider vinegar was a favorite, as was garlic rubbed onto whole grain toast. Cayenne pepper on food was a given to help circulation. Mom would walk around the store holding babies, singing lullabies so new moms could breathe and pick up dinner. Some of those babies are customers today.

Bea (customers rarely called her "Beatrice") carried out groceries. She listened to people's stories about their lives. She listened to our staff who talked to her, too, and she worried about how little retail can afford to pay. She was our best customer and refused a salary as one of our staff. Instead, she insisted I pass hers onto someone who really needed it.

Mom thought of herself as my partner...but she was also my mom. This made for some interesting dynamics (just as Adam and I have today). We talked about almost everything and most of the time we were on the same page. However, when I look back, I realize that I hurt her feelings and made her feel like a third wheel when I showed everyone else on staff our designs for t-shirts. I didn't ask her to look. Didn't ask her if she liked the bright blue or Kelly green. "Who am I? Chopped liver?" springs to mind.

I wish I could re-do some moments. Just like, and I'm not being facetious, I wish I could apologize to her for my silent aggravation and rolling of the eyes when she took heaven to task for making teeth shift after the age of 50. "Food gets stuck between my teeth all the time," she'd state. I get that now. I understand why she'd only have a yogurt for lunch when she worked in the store.

On some subjects, she ruled our roost. We carried no chocolate for years because Mom said we absolutely, positively should not carry chocolate unless it was Fair Trade and organic. The problem was that no organic chocolate existed in those days, and Fair Trade was just a glimmer in someone's eye.

Whenever I fretted that we needed chocolate, because who doesn't love chocolate, to help pay the rent, she threatened a boycott. She would, she said, sing protest songs outside the store. She stood fast on principle.

Chocolate had to be organic because organic meant you followed the rules. Organic meant you couldn't use kids to slave in the fields and then, oh, by the way, not pay them. Organic meant you didn't spray the plants with chemicals. By drawing that line in the sand, Mom insisted we have a conscience and made us and the shop better. And I say that with no irony.

Today there are so many organic and Fair Trade chocolates available that it's hard to choose which ones we should offer in our shop. We have them aplenty at the registers, and I order organic chocolates with arty designs from France for the holidays. Nathan and Tori use organic cocoa powder and organic chocolate chips in our cookies and cakes baked back in the kitchen. We have ready-to-eat products throughout the store that include organic chocolate. Some are raw chocolate, most dark.

Here's a recipe we make every single day in the shop—it's the most requested dessert by folks who use us for catering (We make them into mini-bites). And of course it uses organic chocolate.

Coconut Manna Chocolate Mousse

Serves 12   **use an 8- or 9 inch pie plate**

½ C coconut oil	1 C dark maple syrup
½ C Nutiva coconut manna	2-3 Tbsp vanilla extract
1 C organic cocoa powder	1 C cacao nibs, garnish

In a food processor, using the steel blade, pulse, then blend all the ingredients except the nibs for a minute or two. Spoon into a pie plate, sprinkle with nibs and put into the fridge. Just before serving, cut into wedges to serve. This goes wonderfully with peaches and/or nectarines.

• •

Dairy-free, gluten-free (check your vanilla at home because many vanillas are made with alcohol from wheat), egg-free? Yes. Fat-free? Not even close. But the creamy decadence has health properties too. Here's Adam's bit from an old newsletter:

> But isn't coconut full of saturated fats? Why yes, it is. And aren't saturated fats bad for us? Well, yes and no. It's complicated. But even in a worst-case scenario, where saturated fats are as bad as they're made out to be, none of the research implicating saturated fats in heart disease, etc., has looked specifically at coconuts. This is important because coconuts contain special saturated fats called medium chain triglycerides (MCTs) that are different from other saturated fats in the diet. They're digested differently, they're absorbed differently, they're burned differently, and they're stored differently.
>
> Perhaps the biggest difference is in how the body burns MCTs –very efficiently compared to other fats. This efficiency means two things for us: energy and weight loss. Most "normal" people won't feel especially energized after a meal containing coconut oil, but it does make a difference for endurance athletes and others who burn through energy more quickly. And coconut oil may also give more energy to people with fat malabsorption syndromes.

And yes, coconut oil supports weight loss, too. The key here is the term *diet-induced thermogenesis*, which means "the burning of calories stimulated by a meal." In one study, a meal that got 40 percent of its calories from MCTs doubled the diet-induced thermogenesis of an identical meal that got 40 percent of its calories from regular vegetable oils. In another study, where the "meals" consisted entirely of fats and oils, the MCTs increased diet-induced thermogenesis threefold. And while the vegetable oil raised blood triglycerides by 68 percent, the MCTs had no effect. So much for "artery-clogging" saturated fat!

Of course, coconut oil has calories, and when you sit there eating coconut oil by the spoonful, you're getting more than you're burning. So, for weight loss, coconut oil shouldn't be an *addition* to the diet as much as a *substitution* for oils that are already there.

Mom drew a line in the sand about other ingredients as well. Which is why today she would have conniptions about most of the fresh breads we sell. She would say we've sold out, crossed a line we shouldn't have. That our breads don't nourish.

But it's not our fault.

Look at fresh breads everywhere and I bet you'll find virtually none are 100 percent whole grain. You'll see breads decorated with seeds and that contain some whole grains. But if you read the label, you'll see "wheat flour" as a first or second ingredient, which means white flour. Wheat flour = white flour. Not whole wheat flour. Not whole grain. I don't even know what she would say about the health benefits of the gluten-free breads.

It's not that we want to carry breads that are second-class citizens, it's just that most bakers today tell us it's either too hard to make breads that are 100 percent whole grain, or that if they do, we won't buy them. "People don't like dense, heavy breads," they tell us. "People want airy-fairy, light breads." What Mom and Grandma Sarah used to call "kvatch." Meaning you could squeeze that white bread into a spitball.

Taste is a matter of what we're used to, a matter of education, and I know many of our customers love Dan's Brick Oven Bread. Dan's website says, "Call it artisan. Call it small batch. Call it sustainable, organic, local, naturally leavened, fermented or prebiotic. Use whatever adjective or trendy buzzword you like to describe this bread...but it's food. Real, living food created by the synergy of simple ingredients, biodynamic farming practices and traditional baking techniques."

Dan doesn't advertise, and he makes just enough bread for himself and those who choose to seek it out. And it's 100 percent whole grain. Dan knows the farmers who grow his grains, and he stone mills those grains into flour himself. Good luck getting enough, say I.

Dan, do you have any friends who bake bread?

Our choice today is either to compromise and carry the best of the available fresh bread we can find, or no fresh bread (except Dan's) at all. I know what Bea's answer would have been.

There are times I am glad she isn't alive to see favorite products gone. We can't get her goat's milk ice cream sweetened with honey. The shop has morphed, changed into something she would not always appreciate (with regard to ingredients—she would still love the staff and all the families who come through our doors).

That said, there are things that Mom would love to know. She made these "confections" that we three Stark siblings absolutely adored. Nowadays, I make them with organic cacao powder (organic and Fair Trade, of course). Mom insisted she actually liked them better with carob.

These no-bake, fudge-like confections do your body good. In fact, there's so much goodness here, I don't know where to begin! Let's mention unhulled sesame seeds, which are eaten in some cultures in place of dairy because of their high calcium content (calcium from unhulled, brown sesame seeds is more easily used by our bodies than calcium from milk, and a higher percentage of the calcium contained actually works for us). Two tablespoons of whole sesame seeds give you a third of your daily requirement of magnesium and about a quarter of your daily requirement of calcium.

Read the labels of most tahinis in the markets, and you'll see they used hulled seeds. Without the hulls, these tahinis or sesame seeds contain NO magnesium, and about 2 percent of our daily calcium. Those hulls make a world of difference. (Just like the whole grains in bread make their world of difference). Think of whole sesame seeds as whole grain bread, and hulled seeds as white bread.

Eaten for thousands of years, sesame was thought to possess magical properties, and sesame contains sesamol, which fights rancidity.

Mom's confections make a wonderful, quick breakfast with an apple or pear or bowl of berries, and a cup of tea. They make great hiking food and are a terrific after-school snack. I made them for Adam and Veena (Adam's wife and my lovely, intelligent daughter-in-law), and Veena's mom, Revathy, after Mira was born. They devoured them in the hospital. And I've made them at the library with kids, in schools, and at the Harvey Wheeler Community Center. Kids are nuts about Mom's confections (made with chocolate). If only she knew.

Sometimes, Tori and Nathan (our bakers) make Bea's Confections in the shop's kitchen. They use organic cocoa powder and you can ask that they make a batch if you don't see them in our case. If you're a carob fan, you can request Bea's Confections made that way, too.

Beatrice Stark's Carob or Cocoa Confections

Makes about 42 balls, which keep nicely in the fridge. Yes, use organic ingredients, because you're worth it!

1 C raw, unfiltered honey	1 C unhulled brown sesame seeds
1 C crunchy peanut butter	½ C hemp hearts
1 C cocoa or carob powder	½ C Fearn soy granules*
1 tsp cinnamon powder	1 C hulled sunflower seeds
1 Tbsp real vanilla extract	1 tsp almond extract

Beat honey and nut butter with a wooden spoon until "liquidy." Mix in remaining ingredients. Dough will be sticky, stiff and hard to mix. Persevere! Good exercise for flabby arms.

Pinch off tablespoons of batter and roll in hands. Your chocolate or carob balls will grow glossy. Taste one to make sure you love them. You will! They will taste even better after some hours because the flavors have had the chance to meld.

Fearn soy granules are an old-time product, and our store orders them directly from Fearn because most distributors have forgotten them. They're crunchy and add a ton of protein. Mom also used to stir Fearn soy granules into rice during the last 5 minutes of cooking. The granules absorbed any excess moisture and gave the rice a gourmet taste and appearance. Dinner guests would exclaim, "Oooh. So gourmet. It's delicious!"

• •

We have expanded twice into adjoining spaces when business owners on either side retired. In 2006, after our first expansion, the then-owners of the building, the Demerjians, issued an ultimatum: We had six weeks to purchase the building (minus the condo unit that is today Walden Italian Kitchen) or 98 Commonwealth Avenue would turn into a Chinese restaurant. We would be out of business.

We were lucky that our local bank, Middlesex Savings, and our agent, John McLaughlin, helped us navigate tricky waters and make us the owners of our own destiny. Coming up with the money was tough. We jumped through all the hoops John told us to. We would have studied breakdancing if he'd asked.

In retrospect, buying 4/5 of our condo building was the best thing that could have happened to us. Today, no one can kick us out of our space. We're the only ones who can raise our rent. But even John couldn't get us the whole building, and as we've grown and need room to expand, that's a modern-day problem which we've not been able to solve. Tony, who owns the pizza place, said he'd sell us the 1/5 of our condo for "only" a million and a half.

Above the store, we rent to Healing Essence Center. Jonathan and Kathy Glass are like-minded folks, and it makes us feel happy knowing people are getting stuck with acupuncture needles, being massaged and learning about good foods to eat. Not to mention the fact that Jonathan's book, *Total Life Cleanse*, has him on the national speaker circuit.

Right after we bought 4/5 of the condo, Needle Arts, who was renting one of our units, decided to close. I sold my home in Concord to come up with more money to take down walls, expand the shop and renovate.

Our building is old (early 1900's), and we've found some problems. We knew our floors listed towards the back (you can put a ball down at one end of the building and it will roll to the other end). What we didn't know was that the support beams from the basement to the first and second floors had unceremoniously been lopped off by some bright bulb unclear on the concept of structural integrity. We also discovered three layers of walls in one section of the building used as camouflage to hide fire damage.

Today we have steel poles that hold us up and the fire damage has been fixed. The roof is still wavy. At the town's request, we removed part of a stone wall in the basement that sectioned the basement off. I kid you not, we had a young man chipping away at stone, while lying on his back in a tight crawlspace, for a couple of weeks. He sustained a couple of broken fingers, and I wonder how he's doing today. Is he able to play the piano?

All this digging and learning about the history of our building and West Concord has helped us become part of the community. The fellows over at Phillips carried old radiators down to the basement (what sweethearts!) and regaled us about the days when our building was a men's only bar.

Renovating gave us a chance to put in skylights and 150 little drawers for herbs and spices. We actually put in a produce case and constructed a produce department, so fruits and vegetables have a home. Until then, we only sold produce on Tuesdays, and put everything on folding tables and rolling carts and took over the supplement counter.

In pre-renovation days, Tuesdays were a party in the store. Everyone flooded in to buy organic greens, root vegetables and butternut squash. People would shop for the week and grab apples, onions and garlic along with burdock and shiitake mushrooms. Folks depended on us for their organic produce, because in our early years, you couldn't get organics at Stop & Shop. Which brings back memories of being in Israel and getting an email that our produce truck, instead of delivering that Tuesday to our store in Massachusetts, was wandering in Concord, New Hampshire, lost.

I knew that our customers (and staff) would be distressed, but at the same time, our customers understood. We were so lucky they still loved us! With their help, our staff were able to calm down.

Here's a favorite recipe made with butternut squash from our March 2007 newsletter. Each year we see people coming in with their dog-eared copy around New Year's. It's a perfect recipe for days that are cold and blustery. If you're able to buy peeled and diced organic butternut squash, this dish becomes a five-minute snap to prepare for the oven! Of course you can halve, peel and cube your own squash, or substitute diced yams.

Vegetarian? Substitute a fake sausage—there are many that are pretty terrific.

The savory herbs used here provide complex tones and flavors to dishes, and also have medicinal properties valued since the beginning of time. The word *sage* is derived from the Latin, meaning *health* or *healing powers*. The ancient Greeks and Romans administered sage for everything from snakebite to promoting longevity. And rosemary? In Shakespeare's *Hamlet*, Ophelia says, "There's rosemary, that's for remembrance!" Rosemary's constituents have been shown to inhibit the growth of skin tumors and to provide a natural antioxidant protection against skin cancer.

Thyme is generally used in combination with other remedies as an antiseptic, and in some long-ago wars, thyme was used as a dressing for wounds.

Roasted Sausages with Butternut Squash (or Sweet Potatoes) and Herbs

Serves 4   **Roast at 450 degrees**

6 C cubed, peeled butternut squash	1 tsp dried sage
1 lb Niman bratwurst, each cut into	1 tsp dried thyme
6 pieces	1 tsp dried rosemary
12 garlic cloves, minced	1 tsp black pepper
3 Tbsp extra virgin olive oil (EVOO)	Rosemary as garnish, optional

Preheat oven to 450 degrees.

Toss everything together in a large bowl or mix carefully right in the oven-proof serving platter or shallow roasting pan. Place platter or roasting pan in oven and roast until squash is tender, about 30 minutes. Your sausage will be nicely browned. Amazing how something so simple can taste so good! Isn't this easy?

This is nice served alongside steamed spinach, kale, collards or broccoli. Think color!

• •

But we were speaking of lost trucks and making mistakes while trying to run a business. There's no way I'm going to 'fess up and tell you all the goofs I've made these last thirty years. Some, however, do allow me to see that we've matured and that our business is legit. Some go back far enough that I can laugh.

One story goes "the night before Christmas" on our very first year, December 1989. Adam and I were closing the store. I put the proceeds from the three nights before Christmas in a bank bag (we weren't making enough money to do nightly deposits) and we locked up and went out to the car. It was not a night of heavenly peace. Something had happened, and we were not speaking. The money bag got put on the roof of the car as various and sundry, including dirty linen that I took home and washed, were loaded inside.

Still not speaking, we got in and drove off. We got home and realized we'd forgotten to stop at the bank and put the bank bag in the night deposit drop, and then realized that the bank bag was nowhere to be found. We remembered we'd put it on the roof of the car.

We drove back over our route, over and over and over again. No bank bag. Finally, we called the police. We needed that money to make payroll. Forget about profits. There were none in those days.

Lucky for us, that evening was unseasonably warm. One family was sitting outside on their front porch, instead of going to midnight Mass, I suppose. They heard the metal part of the bank bag clink on the road. Curious, they went into the road to look. They retrieved our bag and called the police.

I was such a newbie and in such a panic that I don't remember which house it was or the name of the family who saved our bacon that night. At the time, I did thank them. I hope I gave them a suitable reward.

Today we're still making all kinds of mistakes.

I'm more prone to dumb mistakes than most. Like not listing ingredients in the right order on our raw juice label (ingredients have to be listed in order of predominance, with the ingredients used in the greatest amount first, followed in descending order by those in smaller amounts). This necessitated a temporary, stick-this-over-the-printed-label label, which we are still using today because I ordered so many glass bottles.

I am also more easily taken in by a fast-talking salesperson who wants to sell me a "Fair Trade item made by handicapped people in Africa" which turns out to be plastic and made on an assembly line in China.

For the most part, Adam and our staff protect me from my own gullible nature and my hot-to-trot, let's do this right now mode of operating.

I believe we're all enjoying ourselves more. How could you not have fun when you get a contingent of Canadian companies visiting to get our advice on how to do business in the US, or when you get to have a food table at the Jazz Festival in Concord? This past year Roxanne and B and Andrew sizzled up falafel.

Whenever Adam and I were having a hard time, as parents and children will, Mom was the one who calmed the waters. She was the only one who could make Adam lean down and give her a hug. We both miss having her in the shop.

In the early days, as the store and Adam were both maturing, I remember his coming around the corner in the supplement department, a gaggle of women in his wake. I heard him say, "Well, I've never experienced menopause myself, but...." He was about 20.

Adam learned about menopause, and we all listened to recitations about bodily functions. More than we could ever have imagined!

In the year before Mom died, she would ask me to take her to Jordan's Furniture, because every time you went in, they gave you a sparkly necklace. She was convinced no one giving out those necklaces would recognize her as she went in, got a necklace, turned around and went out, and then went in again, and again, and again.

She was hell-bent on collecting enough necklaces to bring back to our shop to treat our little ones. Tricking Jordan Furniture was a heck of a lot of fun, she said. Yes, I offered to buy necklaces wholesale, but where was the challenge in that, she said. Eventually Mom bought a chair, so Jordan's got the better of the deal and I didn't feel quite so embarrassed or guilty. Giving those sparkly necklaces out at the shop gave Mom incredible joy.

She died in 2004, and recently one of those kids (now an adult) brought me the sparkly necklace she'd given him. After showing it to me, I watched him proffer it to a new little one, who was just as thrilled to receive it.

Today, social media and emails have added a whole other dimension to our community. Meg puts things up on Instagram. This is part of our history now, too. I've saved some emails and posts for posterity, like this email from Adam:

> "So, John S., one of our customers, long-time Reiki guy, and ginseng aficionado, requested to Facebook-friend me. And, unlike many other customers, he didn't just click, he actually

wrote a quick note, something like 'oh great pill master, grant me my request.' Also, unlike other customers who just random-ly friend me (yes, 'friend' is now a verb...), I like the guy. So, I wrote back, and he thanked the Great Pill Master, and I wrote something about how the student shall become the master, and the master shall become the student, and thus turns the great wheel in the sea of stars throughout eternity.

"Then, dude upped the ante (see below). The point is, to all you non-believers, this is one of the ways Facebook can be fun, be-cause now it's out there for all to see, and I'm SURE some ran-dom friend of his or mine is going to chime in at some point."

John wrote:

"The STARK is my salesman, I shall not want.
He maketh me to try herbs grown in green pastures,
he leadeth me to buy ginseng waters.
He restoreth my adrenals;
he leadeth me in the paths of nutritiousness
for my frame's sake.
Yea, though I walk through the valley
of the bottles of pills,
I will fear no evil;
for thou art with me,
thy Mom and her staff, they counsel me.
Thou preparest a purchase before me
in the presence of my free radicals;
thou anointest my head with fish oil;
my Qi runneth over.
Surely goodness and healthiness shall follow me

all the days of my life;
and I will shop in the house of the STARK forever."

I'm not adept at social media. When I got hacked on Facebook and my friends got a video showing them how they could melt belly fat, I had no idea how to disavow the video. And it took people emailing me and calling me at home to find out that Adam had posted an April Fool's joke on the store's Facebook page.

"BREAKING NEWS! **April 1, 2019**: a leaked copy of the full 400-page Mueller Report reveals overwhelming evidence of an illicit link between the current administration and community natural foods store owner and 2015 US Retailer of the Year Debra Stark. Cash, truckloads of organic kale, fair trade Doritos, and borderline illegal herbal "stamina" supplements were all funneled to fund opposition research during the 2016 campaign in clear violation of campaign finance laws.

"'What vitamin lady?' said the president. 'I don't know a vitamin lady. I mean, I like vitamins. Don't get me wrong. Don't you like vitamins? American vitamins. I guarantee I like vitamins as much, actually more than, really anyone—really everyone—in history. Big, strong vitamins.'

"In an impromptu press conference later in the day, presidential spokesperson Sarah Huckabee Sanders categorically denied that the president liked vitamins.

"Meanwhile, closer to home, Senator Elizabeth Warren (D-MA) issued a statement through her office. 'I am disappointed in Debra. That's the last time we'll have her cater my events.'

"Finally, reached for comment in her home in Acton, Debra Stark quickly pointed out that it was April Fool's Day, thus FAKE NEWS, and hung up on this reporter."

Adam loves the shop. I believe he decided our work was his work, instead of going off to medical school, because of Grace Pintabona and Mary Kadlik. They were his mentors. When I told our staff that Adam was officially a co-owner, I said how grateful I was because I'd always felt that I had two children, Adam and the shop, and the thought that one of them would not continue when I was gone made me feel bereft.

It has been soul-satisfying to see Adam help grow the business and watch him grow right along with it. It's a relief that I'm not flying solo, that I don't have to worry by myself about how we'll pay for a new floor or expand our physical space. But on nights when I imagine both Adam and I are staring at the ceiling, sleepless, I feel guilty. What have I done to my kid? His life could have been easier, and he could have made big bucks doing something else. (The same goes for all our staff.)

But the next day, the sun comes out. All seems right with the world. We work with interesting people who make us roll in the aisles. A customer comes in with a box of blueberries from her garden. My bones settle and my feet feel part of the earth. I know that both of us are exactly where we are meant to be.

Mom and Pop would be proud of us. Over wonton soup and Peking duck (Adam and Pop) and Buddha's delight (on the lighter side, no sugar, no cornstarch, no MSG) for Mom and me at Chang An's, we'd talk about everything. This weekly tradition meant a lot. I miss it. I mourn the fact that my parents can't see Adam and his family or our shop as it is today.

Adam and the next gens in the store bring their intelligence, humor and hard work as they carry us forward. I love watching them stretch their wings.

We Starks, Adam and Debra, cherish our extended family, one that has grown to include so many people. It feels rich, abundant and satisfying. We know that every day is still about earning trust.

Trust is especially important in a shop like ours, still regarded by many as "fringe." I try to keep in mind the joke (who's the author?) my father used to tell Mom to keep her on her toes: "I used to eat a lot of natural foods until I learned that most people die of natural causes." That reminds me not to get too cocky.

Chapter 5

Getting Myself Into Trouble:
Behind The Scenes While Running A Store

You think running a shop is simple? Turn on lights, buy a register, put some eggs in the fridge and open sesame! But I can tell you now that running a store is a lot more than just paying for inventory like coconut water, LSD and aspirin.

Okay. Hah. We've got no magic mushrooms or aspirin. And sales of coconut water seem to be waning. But reading trends and riding the wave can be great fun…unlike adhering to rules and regs.

Some rules and regulations seem just nutty, but woe unto the shop that doesn't toe the line. It hasn't helped that I've always thought my own internal rules and regs were eminently reasonable, sometimes made more sense, and therefore…well, you get the picture.

There are still days when I wonder how on earth I ever thought it was smart to open a store. In the olden days, I used to get under the covers after long days at the shop. I'd have a spoon, two pints of ice cream (organic, of course) and two bags of potato chips (also organic). I would drown my sorrows in calories. I'd eat a pint of ice cream, then cleanse the palate with chips. Another pint of ice cream. Another bag of chips. I'd sleep like a dead person until the next morning when the merry-go-round would start again. But shall I tell you some of the ways I got myself and our shop into trouble?

Bathrooms. In 1989, right after we opened, I was told by the Concord Board of Health that we needed a second bathroom in our 1,200 square foot store. We had a handful of staff and another small handful of customers. I was told that we needed that second bathroom because men and women couldn't share. Naively, I asked, "What do people do at home? What about co-ed dorms?"

Those two questions caused more than a year of pain because they were taken as a challenge to authority. As part of my punishment, we were forced to spend $3,000 on the installation of a toilet and sink for our male staffers (male customers could, apparently, use the same bathroom as women customers and female staffers).

The bathroom was installed in the basement. It looked something like a solitary confinement cell. What's more, the town sewer regularly backed up into that toilet and flooded the basement. After ten years, we had it sealed off. I don't think anyone ever used it, the health inspector who told us we had to install it left her job, and no health inspector since has asked why men and women use the same bathroom in our store. But it taught me an important lesson: that one does not mess with rules or regulations.

Eggs. We have refrigerators and freezers. They use lots of energy, and they are always breaking down. Our small shop paid $30,000 dollars last year to Hub Electric for maintenance and repairs. Holy Toledo!

Which begs the question, why do we, in the good old USA, keep eggs in the refrigerator when so much of the world does not? (Joke: Why shouldn't you tell an egg a joke? Answer: Because it might crack up!)

Much of the rest of the world sells eggs at room temperature. Eggs are displayed as they came out of the chicken, feathers and goop and all. The eggs are not washed. This is as nature intended, because the chicken pushes the egg out coated with a substance that not only keeps it fresh, but protects it, and us, against contamination.

We remove this coating by washing eggs in hot water with detergent, instead of trusting the chicken. She's been doing this a lot longer than we have, and I, for one, am okay with some feathers on my eggs. They'd make wonderful compost for the garden.

I believe that I'm the only one who would lobby for eggs au naturelle, so I don't utter a word on this subject in the shop. But there are times when I stare at the refrigerated egg case.

Potlucks. Apparently, potlucks are illegal in the state of Massachusetts. Who knew? We certainly didn't, and we learned the hard way. We announced a cooking contest and potluck in our store newsletter and put up signs on our doors. People were psyched. I had my own dish, a ratatouille with add-ins like Fakin' Bacon tempeh, at home in my own fridge.

The day before the event, people were wildly excited. There was buzz going on in the store. But then we were abruptly informed that we could have no potluck. No hoi polloi bringing food from home. Potlucks were verboten, and the ban would be strictly enforced.

Should I have known that there was a law against potlucks? Yes. But potlucks had been a part of our history since opening. There was extreme panic when the day before our event we learned we'd have to come up with a Plan B. You would have been proud at the grace with which our kitchen stepped into the breach and saved the day. We treated 200 people to a garlicky green salad with goat cheese and vegetarian chili, cornbread and a homemade dessert. It looked easy breezy to our customers who came sans their homemade offerings.

The dessert we might have served may have been one of my favorites, my mom's walnut surprise cookies. These were the first cookies my brothers and I learned to make growing up, and they're still our favorite. If I had to choose one cookie recipe to use over and over, this would be the one.

Never mind the fancy desserts–these unprepossessing cookies are delicious and always a hit. No matter what flavor you choose to make them, it's the basic formula that works so well. I love the fact that no matter which variation, all it takes is a bowl, a wooden spoon and a strong arm.

Check out our third cookbook, *The Blue Ribbon Edition: From Our Kitchen To Yours* for variations on this formula, some of which are definitely gluten-free.

When I want to make the recipe gluten-free, I substitute almond meal, pecan meal or any ground nut flour for the whole wheat pastry flour. I've made them gluten-free, too, by using desiccated coconut instead of flour.

The gluten-free versions made this way are more crumbly, but I bet adding a tablespoon of psyllium husks would correct that. If I need to bake something nut-free, well, it's easy to substitute currants or date pieces for the walnuts.

How to present these cookies? Mom used to bake them in an 8x8 pan and cut them into squares. I think they look better when patted into a pie plate, baked and then cut into pie-shaped wedges. Wedges look more interesting when compared to other cookies. You can serve with chocolate mousse and fresh berries, fresh pineapple or ice cream, or serve plain with a cup of tea.

Nowadays, I always add some chocolate chips to my batter!

Mom's Walnut Surprise Cookies

Serves 8-12, Bake at 350 degrees and use a pie plate or 8x8 pan

1 C coconut sugar	½ C whole wheat pastry flour
1 egg	¼ tsp sea salt
2 Tbsp pure vanilla extract	1 C walnuts, coarsely chopped
	1 C organic chocolate chips

Preheat oven to 350 degrees. Grease the pie plate or 8x8 brownie pan.

In a small bowl, beat together the sugar, egg and vanilla with a wooden spoon until "liquidy." Mix in flour and salt. Add walnuts (and chocolate chips, if using) and mix well. Batter *will be* sticky and hard to mix. Spoon batter into pie plate or pan. Pat out (easier to do with wet hands).

Bake cookies in preheated oven for 20 minutes, or until lightly brown and edges slightly pull away from the sides of the pie plate or pan. Remove pie plate or pan from oven and place on cooling rack for 10 minutes. While cookies are still warm, cut into 12 pie wedges or 12 squares. NOTE: Cut while still warm or you won't be able to cut at all. These cookies are best eaten the day they are made, but they freeze beautifully.

• •

But potlucks. I always thought they were the greatest way to bring people together, to create community, to make non-profit fundraisers lively. To make school and faith meetings fun. There's historical precedence for enjoying public potlucks. Wasn't the original potluck called Thanksgiving?

But the law states that "No foods for a public event or fundraiser should be made in a home kitchen (except baked goods such as cookies, brownies or cakes). A bake sale is the only public event that does not require a temporary permit."

Why did potlucks get the axe? Our tax dollars decreed that because home kitchens are not inspected and not licensed, food made in home kitchens can be dangerous. We might kill each other with food brought from home. It's a possibility. We might also get hit by a bus crossing the road, but I haven't seen buses banned.

Historically, how many people have died at church potlucks? I don't re-call cases of murder by potluck reported on TV. And if our home food isn't good enough to share with neighbors, is it safe enough to feed our kids? Shouldn't we ban homecooked meals altogether? Just following the logic here.

Today I think of the Northeast Organic Farm Association (NOFA) who used to have wonderful potlucks where people brought their own place settings, together with a covered dish. I remember a Slow Food Boston potluck held in a church in Arlington with a lecture on the his-tory of beans. The potlucks we used to hold in the store were wonder-ful. Dishes prepared with love and imagination were brought to share (no macaroni and mayo dishes at our potlucks). Our potlucks were the best, and I miss them.

Gloves. When you run a business, there are costs you would never have imagined, like thousands of dollars each year for latex and vinyl gloves. We would prefer to use that money to buy a purple Cadillac van for catering. But as of 1999, it's the law, so we glove up to handle food.

Personally, I don't want my food handled with plastic, but that's an-other issue.

The law says gloves protect us from spreading microbes better than washing hands with soap and water. Those gloves get stripped off any time one of our staff stops to serve a soup. Then we re-glove to resume chopping a carrot. We re-glove after answering the telephone or giving out hugs. We re-glove to bag lettuce. When we put dried fruit into bags.

I don't know how our staff get anything done since taking off and putting on gloves is not easy. I can't put on a pair of gloves to save my life. My fingers won't go in the right slots. Especially if my hands are wet, because the law says one must wash hands before putting on gloves. That's why our staff won't allow me in the kitchen in the store anymore. That's why I'm not allowed to bag spinach.

Yes, Roxanne Bispham, our lovely kitchen manager, did try and show me how to blow into a glove to make it inflate and then easier to put on. But aren't I then contaminating my hand and my glove both with germs? Just asking.

Behind the scenes, I wonder if anyone has calculated how many millions of disposable gloves are dumped at American landfills each year? Call me crazy, but how does gloving protect John Q. Public when a cook, wearing gloves, pushes his hair away from his eyes or scratches his nose? Does a glove protect us when "Smithy" takes out the trash and comes back into the kitchen, gloves still on, and dishes out lamb lentil stew? Wearing gloves doesn't necessarily mean the person wearing them is going to use good hygiene.

I've seen people in a cheese emporium wearing their gloves to cut cheese, and then casually scratch their crotch. Am I allowed to say that here? But the real question is, does that person realize they have to take off those gloves, wash their hands and re-glove?

We have hand sinks (sinks that are reserved only for washing hands because you're not allowed to wash hands in the same sink you use to wash lettuce). But what would happen if we just washed hands and forgot the gloves? I know all the companies that make gloves would go out of business, and their employees would need to look for jobs in another industry. But aside from that, would we be endangering public health?

Plastic Packaging. In our shop, we obsess about replacing plastic packaging, particularly for take-out from our kitchen. If only everything was in glass. If only our deli could serve everything in returnable mason jars.

I guess we *could* use mason jars to package all our grab and go food, but then our customers would have to carry around all that heavy glass. They'd develop carpal tunnel syndrome. That's the downside. And we'd have to build a new room for storing glass jars and lids. And have another dishwasher to sanitize jars returned to us. The upside is that we would sell a lot more arnica for overused and sore muscles and joints.

Here's a soup we can imagine going into a glass jar, if we were to use those. Maybe you will make it and put it in old glass jars you have at home. It's perfect for January, when the days are dark, and the nights are darker still. If you've splurged at the holidays and need help paying bills, try soothing both soul and pocketbook with good food like soup. I always say that you can feed an army on a handful of lentils. This pot of soup will feed *your* army, or you, with leftovers in containers to pop in the freezer for next week and the week after. How much does this soup cost to make using all organic ingredients? About $10 for the whole pot, or $1.25–$1.50 per serving. Cost fluctuates with the price of veggies.

Did you know that lentils are composed of **26 percent protein**, one of the highest levels of protein from any plant-based food after soybeans and hemp? Lentils are eaten in many countries daily, sometimes spooned over rice.

Pay-the-Mortgage Lentil Soup

Serves 8

1½ C red lentils	14 C water or veg stock*
1½ C brown lentils	1 tsp marjoram
¾ C barley or brown rice	1 tsp ground cumin
8 cloves garlic, minced	1 Tbsp good salt
4 medium carrots, diced, about 4 C	1 tsp black pepper
4 stalks celery, sliced, about 4 C	4 C chopped spinach or kale

This recipe follows my characteristically simple formula for soup: throw everything in a pot, bring to a slow boil, lower heat to lowest, cover pot and simmer. In this case, simmer the soup for about 2 hours. Perfect to make on a Sunday morning when you're reading the newspaper. Stir in chopped greens during the last 5-10 minutes of cooking. Give your soup a good stir and once the greens are cooked, serve it in bowls, or let it cool and then refrigerate it to save it for the next day. Or portion it out to bring to work.

Depending upon your pot, you may need to add more water. I cooked mine in a pot whose lid didn't fit tightly, and the water steamed out, so I had to add two more cups of water as the soup simmered. I'll use a different pot next time, but in case your pot is like mine... Can you add a ham bone? Yes, but I like this soup vegetarian, just as it is!

To date, we've not found containers that aren't mason jars or plastic that showcase a couscous chickpea salad with feta and olives in the deli case. People want to see what they're buying. No one wants to buy a pig in a poke. We know because we've tried cardboard boxes. Not only would food soak through the boxes, but, yes, sales tanked because folks couldn't see what our pumpkin seed-tomatillo dip looked like.

There are containers out there today made from genetically modified corn, but that's not an option in our shop. If we can put a man on the moon, why can't we make a see-through food-service container that doesn't harm the planet?

Our customers worry about this. We worry about this. Which is why I was heartened to read that Sandra Pascow Ortiz, a researcher in Mexico, is experimenting with cactus leaves to make an edible, biodegradable plastic. She's hoping plastic from cactus will replace single-use cutlery or shopping bags. Someday.

Wooden Cutting Boards (versus plastic ones). The law, as written today, says that we must use plastic cutting boards in our kitchen.

All my cutting boards at home are wood. But Massachusetts health regulations mandate plastic cutting boards because they are "sanitary." When I asked about this, our health inspector encouraged me to go to the state legislature and "Work to change the law!" She was right, but there are so many laws I'd like to change (remember eggs and potlucks?) that I might get a reputation for being that lady, the one with the shop in Concord that was always being a pest. A health food version of the cat lady.

And, no dummy I, I remember the two years it took to help change a town law so we could replace the gold lettering running along the bottom of our windows that said, "Eat Well Be Happy–Eat Well Be Happy–Eat Well Be Happy." A lovely decorative runner.

What was the town's objection, you ask? It seems our decorative runner pushed us outside the allowable limits for number of words or amount of window real estate we were allowed. This despite the fact that our runner had been there since we opened in 1989. Despite the fact it was decorative whimsy in keeping with the town's aesthetics.

But when we replaced old window panes, we were told we couldn't replace our beloved Eat Well Be Happy along the bottom of the windows —until I got that law changed two years later.

Can you imagine how long it would take to change a state health code law that would allow wooden cutting boards?

For the record, plastic cutting boards are not more sanitary, nor safer. Wooden cutting boards, no matter if yours is a new wooden board or one you've chopped on for years, kill bacteria.

Dr. Dean Otis Cliver, who retired in 2007 (and who has since died), was a 30-year veteran of food safety science who worked for the U.S Biological Laboratories Food Research Institute, and University of Wisconsin's Department of Bacteriology. He published a series of articles on plastic and wooden cutting boards, and he found that 99.9 percent of salmonella, listeria and e coli, all bacteria that cause serious illness, died after three minutes when placed on wooden cutting boards. His tests were conducted on seven different species of trees and four types of plastic. No bacteria died on plastic.

A couple of years ago, our kitchen was written up for more than a dozen "serious" violations, each one of which was a single plastic cutting board that had dings and scratches. Tell me, how do you cut on a cutting board without leaving scratches?

Raw Milk. I know most folks believe raw milk is dangerous, but my mother believed it was healthier than pasteurized milk. She said if barns were kept clean, if cows were kept clean, their udders washed as she used to wash them when she worked on the Whitney estate during World War II, pasteurization, which kills good and bad microbes both, would not be necessary. Mom said the barns on the Whitney estate were so clean you could eat off the floors, and that cars lined up for miles and people brought their own bottles to get rich, wonderful raw milk.

Yep, we know it's illegal to sell raw milk in any retail establishment in MA. We don't break the law. But when a raw milk buying club was using our parking lot to distribute raw milk, we were told we ran the risk of having our store shut down. The buying club moved elsewhere.

Supplements and the FDA. If you were to open a golf pro shop, or a shop that sells fabric, you'd be safe from controversy. Not so with supplements.

Mom gave us supplements growing up. And I was the champ, I could swallow a handful all at once. I believe my record was 23 capsules down the hatch with one swallow of liquid. Watching me made my brothers gag.

However, The Food and Drug Administration (FDA) repeats, over and over again, to news reporters, to television interviewers, to anyone who will listen, that we are an unregulated industry and that supplements may be dangerous. They say it so often that people believe it's true (fake news).

It isn't true. In 1994, Congress passed the Dietary Supplement Health Education Act (DSHEA) which formally and officially gave the FDA the power to regulate. The FDA can say a label doesn't cut mustard. They can have products pulled off our shelves. They can declare an ingredient persona non grata, and they can shut a company down.

Jerry (not his real name) asked me why the FDA keeps repeating that supplements aren't regulated. The simple answer, I think, is politics and money. Every FDA director and most FDA top scientists have come from the drug industry. Supplements are an economic threat to the drug industry. In my opinion, that's it in a nutshell.

In 2019, the federal government said that because CBD from hemp has been approved as a drug, Epiodilex, CBD is not allowed in food or drink. This despite the fact that hemp CBD has been consumed safely for years.

I'm suggesting that we just keep stating that the FDA has the power to regulate and protect. Maybe the press will hear us. So, yes, the FDA has the power to regulate and protect us under DSHEA. Real news.

Politicians. I bet most shops don't care what their elected officials eat. We do! We vote for politicians who will protect us, and who are smart and kind. But we want our leaders to lead by example, and for me, at least, that means eating right, too. You bet your bippy it does. Yet what our politicians eat on the campaign trail is far from healthy. I enjoyed writing this romp on an earlier presidential campaign.

Can you judge a presidential candidate by what he eats on the campaign trail? This food expert says "yes!"

One craves Fritos, Cheez Doodles and cotton candy, and the other chomps on chocolate chip cookies and washes them down with milkshakes! This health nut says no wonder their hands shake and they sometimes fumble when trying to answer simple questions. Too much junk food fogs the mind. No wonder one of them needs an afternoon nap and the other needs more energy!

These guys get an F in nutrition. Instead of worrying about chemical weapons they can't find, maybe they should pay attention to the chemicals in their breakfast. Maybe they ought to eat watermelon or an ear of boiled corn instead of cotton candy at the county fair.

What difference does it make if the leader of the free world lives on Twinkies washed down with Diet Coke? The answer is do we want the leader of the free world with a shaky finger on the trigger? Do we want a leader to sign off on ketchup as one of the five fruits and veggies we're supposed to eat each day!?!

Plastic Water Bottles. We're so proud that our town, Concord, Massachusetts, was the first town in the country to ban single-serve plastic water bottles.

I remember my mother saving glass jars and filling them with our well water. Those bottles went everywhere with us with a little rag cloth tied around the neck of the bottle in case we dribbled or there were other unexpected spills. There was no expectation that we could go into a shop and buy a bottle of whatever. Heavens to Betsy!

Everything, for me, circles back to Mom. The store brings back so many memories of her strong convictions on fair labor practices, fresh food as an unalienable right and enriching soil. Plastic cutting boards and food-service gloves weren't an issue in her day, and I wonder what she would say about them now?

Chapter 6

Our Dee-Lightful Sometimes Funny Customers

Our customers buy more almonds and eat more kale than the average American, and we love them for it! They believe the old adage, garbage in garbage out, and eat great food with joy to keep their internal computer humming. Our shoppers are creative cooks but also love their quinoa hemp tabouli from our kitchen, and they want their straight-up chicken, too, because they know our chickens are fine birds and don't do drugs. (Shelton's Turkey established trademark protection for *"Our Chickens and Turkeys Don't Do Drugs"* in 1924. Years ago, sampling Stark Sisters Granola out in California, my table was right next to Shelton's, and, yes, we carry Shelton's products in our store.)

We know our customers want what they want, like sun blocks approved by the Environmental Working Group (EWG) that use mineral ingredients from the earth. They trust us to help them mitigate allergies and stop hot flashes. They want to tell us that Adam's awful-tasting Immune Dragon Superbrew with lomatium did kick their cold or flu to Timbuktu. And that the latest delivery of peaches were extra juicy.

They shop for local foodstuffs in our shop, but also get pleasure buying scarves from repurposed silk saris made in cooperatives in India. Our shoppers get excited when we find goods that tell stories about faraway places like Les Moulins Mahjoub shakshuka from a family estate in Tunisia.

The old-fashioned health food nut wore Birkenstocks and had hairy legs. In the sixties you'd see wrap-around skirts and guys in Hawaiian shirts and ponytails. Not so much nowadays. Today, people come through our doors dressed for teaching school, after working shifts at Emerson Hospital, before or after playing golf or tennis. They come from labs or classrooms at MIT and Harvard. Our customers are police, moms and dads with their little ones, millennials, employees of Vibram Fivefinger shoes, the staff of American Promise (working to get big money out of politics), local high-techs, low-techs and folks with tattoos.

In the growing season, we have farmers who buy prepared food from our kitchen because they are consumed by work in their fields growing food for the rest of us, too busy to nourish themselves. We have little ones wearing feathers and sequins and t-shirts with their favorite animal or superhero. But all our customers, no matter who they are, are no shrinking violets. They tell us exactly what they think. They call us on the carpet when we displease. The topics and opinions vary.

"I have been a faithful customer for many years now and I feel that I must voice my concern over Adam's latest newsletter. I do look forward to them every month and pass them along to family and friends, but I have to tell you I was upset to read this month's letter and Adam's disparaging comment about Rush Limbaugh. A health newsletter is no place for political comments. Not everyone in Concord or MA for that matter are liberal democrats, and I am proud to say that I am that conservative who listens to talk radio. Thank you for listening. All the best, K."

We do listen, and it matters to us that at the end of the day, everyone feels heard and respected. It matters that at the end of the day, our customers still enjoy our company, which they do because they know we like them. We find topics other than politics to talk about!

Of course, the email below is easier to receive.

"Dear Debra, I am a fan of independent business in general, but the environment in the store is truly beyond compare. The staff is knowledgeable—happy to share, committed to service—and are each unique individuals who don't feel pressed to change who they are while they are at work. I like that. There is something else too. I can't even put my finger on it, but you have made my life and the life of my family better, easier, more authentic to who we are. I want specifically to say that we recently had a party catered by the deli. The food was unbelievably good—seriously—people LOVED IT!!! And Roxanne and Alyssa were so helpful and caring. Ah! That's one aspect of the intangible thing—partnership. There is a spirit of partnership that runs through the place that is so nourishing, encouraging and counter to the current trend of business. This is part of what makes Debra's an oasis of humanness!"

Our shoppers are smart cookies. They know to store spices in a cool, dark cupboard. They know not to put tomatoes in the fridge, that avocados and bananas ripen at room temp, that you don't keep chicken in the fridge for months. Yet there's always the odd person out who makes a doozy of a mistake.

One of our habitués returned multiple sticky, plastic bags with grains that were crawling with worms. She wanted a refund. I was horrified. I asked how long she'd had them and where she'd stored them. She freely admitted they were more than a year old and that she'd been keeping them in a cupboard above her stove. I keep all my grains in the freezer, I told her, and we quarantine grains in our walk-in freezer for 72 hours before we ever put them out in bins to make sure they're copacetic. I explained that we couldn't take them back.

Later that day, I found her bags of grains shoved behind goods on our shelves. The tops of the bags were open to release the critters, not into the wild or to feed chickens, but to crawl around our store. Such was her vengeance.

But we know that almost all our customers are in our corner. They make our days in the shop fly. They bring flowers and balloons. They bring humor, wit, affection and sadness.

We have families come into the store after a loved one died because their father or sister delighted in our store and they wanted to remember him or her in a favorite setting. This tugs at our hearts. We have customers who get home and realize they've been so involved in a conversation at the register that they've forgotten to give us a check. They come back in with it the next day.

Then there are stories that haunt us. There is Martha, who we adored. She was always kind, interested in our lives, and now looking back we can see that she always gently deflected questions about her own. We didn't know she was, in her last days, living in her car...until she didn't have that car. We didn't know that she'd rejected help from others in her faith community. She was proud, and we didn't know she couldn't afford the treats she bought from our kitchen. She used money given her by others to spend in our shop.

One day she simply filled her pockets with stones and walked into the Concord River.

To this day we are anguished, and I wonder whether she would have accepted a job in our shop. I often wanted to ask her if she'd work with us, but I never did. I kept holding back because I feared she might be offended.

Martha was the kind of person we relish: she was smart, quick, lively in discourse. Those who read her journals after her death confirmed that in life, she didn't let people get close. It irked her to accept monetary help. In her journal, she wrote about our store, mentioned our staff. Could I, could we have prevented her death and enriched our community at the same time? We'll never know.

We were honored to have Jenny Phillips, who died swimming from a sailboat to shore off Nantucket, as a guest in our shop. Jenny was many things to many people. We knew her as a fierce human rights activist with an unerring sense of right and wrong. A writer, a filmmaker. A wife and a mother. Her interest in others was always intense, up close and personal. Because of Jenny, we work with the Concord prison's work release program.

Bert used to do handstands in our store. Pete used to bring in our cookbooks with Post-it notes so he wouldn't forget to buy the right ingredients for recipes he planned to make. Oscar sang opera when he came in, and Madeline tap-danced. We had a fellow who played the fiddle for Early Bird one year.

We are lucky to have so many lively, funny customers. And then there are customers who don't mean to be funny, but who are. We'll never forget Lydia (not her real name) who in the early days, flew into the store, distraught, and dashed up to Mary Kadlik and me. We were in the kitchen making red lentil and ginger soup, or maybe it was split pea.

She blurted out, "My doctor sent me in for euthanasia." To which, Mary, whom I knew as a very proper New England lady, responded, "Oh honey, it can't be that bad!" I don't know whether I cracked up hardest at Lydia or Mary.

I found out recently that not everyone knows what euthanasia is. Look it up and you'll see why we laughed. What this customer wanted, of course, was echinacea, and yes, we carry that.

At present, there's a couple I need to speak to who are way too lovey-dovey in our store. Think of two humans pantomiming leeches. I heard one of our staff mutter, "Get a room!" Another staffer calls them the "gropsters." If you see them entwined next to the pet food, please come get me.

One story I love is about the shopper who came into the store for Dragon's Blood. "But I worry about the dragons. I'm also vegetarian," she added.

Adam looked at her to see if she were serious. She was. He cautiously explained that Dragon's Blood is a resin from a tree in South America. "But how do I know that what's in this formula is what you're talking about, and not *actual* dragon's blood," she responded. I believe there was a heartfelt pause. "Because actual dragons don't actually exist," said Adam.

"Ahh," she said, "I *think* I see what you're saying."

There was more back and forth. Finally, Adam, in silence, handed her the bottle of Dragon's Blood. So, yes, we carry Dragon's Blood, and from what we hear, the dragons are just fine.

Then there's Gerry (not her real name). For more than 28 years, she's been calling the store. Is she a regular customer? No. Why, you ask, does she keep calling? The scenario goes like this:

Phone rings. I happen to pick up. There's a querulous voice on the other end who doesn't identify herself. I know it's Gerry.

"Say, aren't dried apricots supposed to have vitamin A?"

"Gerry?" I say.

"Yes, oh I was hoping I'd get someone else. Oh well. But don't dried apricots have vitamin A? I got some at the supermarket and they're from Turkey and they only list 2 percent vitamin A on the label."

The reason Gerry doesn't want to get me on the phone is because she knows I'm going to suggest, as I have for years, that she telephone the place where she bought her apricots. "Gerry, if you got the apricots at Shaw's, please ask them."

"I did," she replies. "I spoke to four people there, and no one knows anything. I call your store because you know everything."

We don't know everything, and sometimes we feel helpless, too. An example of this was a young man with bipolar disorder, who was terrified a friend was being abused. He was sure her life was in danger. And he'd lost his cell phone and couldn't reach her because his phone had all his contacts. In an absolute panic, he remembered she shopped in our store. He called us and insisted we find her. He demanded we call the police. We did call the police, and they reached her, and she called him, but it was a rough few days.

We have customers who are often on a mission to do good. One client was a recent "Shop Local!" convert. She was determined to buy veggies only grown in Massachusetts, or New Hampshire or Vermont. "Why are you selling organic romaine lettuce from California?" she demanded. It was January. We looked outside. It was snowing hard and there were two feet of snow on the ground. Alex Gardner, our produce manager tried to explain, "It's just too cold for lettuce to grow here now."

She left sans lettuce, in a huff. She returned like the swallows to San Juan Capistrano in late March. A little early, still, for local romaine. What did she eat in her two-month absence?

Of course, we try to source local because we want to support local agriculture (sustainable and organic, yes, please!). But no matter how hard our local farmers try they won't be able to grow avocados or pineapples because they're just not New England crops.

Our customers go gaga when something is trending on a cooking show or touted by a #1 *New York Times* bestselling author. Anthony William is an example. He wrote *Medical Medium Celery Juice: The Most Powerful Medicine of Our Time,* which recommends that people start their day by drinking 16 ounces of straight celery juice on an empty stomach. This requires an entire head of celery juiced (hopefully, leaves and all). I tried this for a couple of weeks, and found that celery juice is refreshing, really does quench thirst, and is easy to drink. Miracles notwithstanding, I did feel great.

The point is, Anthony Williams has persuaded millions of people to juice celery, and among those millions, many of our customers. As a result, celery (particularly organic celery) is hard to get. It's skyrocketed in price, and bunches of celery are being harvested and rushed to market before they're fully grown in the field.

We wish farmers could snap their fingers and harvest huge heads of organic celery to meet demand. We know trends start (and stop) in the blink of an eye. Take Brussels sprouts. Most of our customers recognize how lucky we are to have organic partners in countries like

Mexico, who jumped in to grow organic Brussels sprouts when this veggie achieved cult status. Today, we still sell more Brussels sprouts than the former favorite American vegetable, green beans.

Leaving vegetables for a moment, you already know that we get asked all kinds of questions. Some unusual. Some startling.

To wit: recently a gentleman asked for "Dick" spray. We're pretty unflappable. Really. The staff in the line of fire adopted a casual stance. Should they look, should they ask what for? Was this a case of a tropical disease that afflicted a specific body part? Should they say, "Excuse me?" to make sure they'd heard correctly? We do have people ask about extremely personal matters. But we never had anyone ask for "Dick" spray.

I think there was a moment or two of respectful, reverential silence. There may have been a discreet question.

The man threw up his hands. "Dicks! You know those little bugs in the yard that give people Lyme disease." I was told that we made him a happy camper when we put a tick repellent in his hand. Everyone made sure to look into his eyes as he walked to the register.

And speaking of heading to the register, there's the rare bird who doesn't. Now, I bet there isn't a kid in the world who hasn't taken a toy, a pencil with a rubber eraser, or some balloons, without his or her parents knowing. In my case, when I was in kindergarten, I took a pair of shiny red doll shoes from Woolworth's. I wanted those tiny red shoes for my doll. I knew that if I asked Pop to buy them for me, the answer would be "No." So I took matters into my own hands. I don't remember exactly how I felt, except I lusted over those shoes. And I knew it was wrong to take them.

The shoes were discovered, and Pop and I went back to Woolworth's. We asked for the manager. I had to apologize and hand the red shoes back. I can still feel the heat of my shame. The Woolworth's manager, however, was bored because, I guess, he'd seen many little girls pocketing doll shoes.

The same happens in our store. Little hands can't resist a piece of candy or a glittery crystal. We always tell children we understand and remember how we, ourselves, were once tempted. We are kind because of our own memories. We feel for these children who often stand there, like we once did, lower lip quivering.

On the other hand, I think we can all expect adults to control those impulses. MaryJane Wuensch, otherwise affectionately known as MJ, who has worked in the store since she and Bernie hiked the Alps years ago, watched a woman stroll the aisles, fill her canvas shopping bag and then head out our back door. MJ, fearless, went out after her and said, "Miss. So sorry you had trouble finding the register. Let me show you where it is." MJ is persuasive, and the woman returned with her to the shop. The rung total of the women's bag was over $200 dollars. We have to sell about a ton of oats to cover that kind of loss.

We thought Betty (not her real name) was a gem. She had a quiet, genteel voice. She always seemed happy as a clam in our store. When she went on our radar, we felt like dolts. It had taken years to flag her because she was an aberration. We have so many honest and lovely people who come through our doors, who feel like family.

Suffice it to say, Betty had many tricks up her sleeve and was a brilliant thief. The five-finger discount was her friend. For us, the straw that broke the camel's back was a simple catch in the supplement department. I was helping another customer and looked over to see she'd come back into the store after shopping. She had her two grocery bags on the floor in front of her. She had a vitamin bottle tucked into each armpit. I watched as she moved to drop those bottles into her bags. She saw me and knew that I'd seen her. She put both bottles back onto the shelves.

We wrote her a no-trespass order. She answered my simple, no examples, no accusations letter with wonder. Mystification, she said. She wanted to know if it was because she'd dropped bay leaves on the floor. To this day, I see her around town, which is uncomfortable. Occasionally she will approach me and say she wishes me well. I wonder where she is shopping. Who is she ripping off?

Yes, we spend a lot of time listening and conversing with our customers, and many of those interactions take place back in the supplement department. We get asked how to make a sore throat better, whether probiotics might help tummy problems, whether magnesium will help relieve leg cramps (it will!) We get asked about concussions (we have a handout) and broken bones (another handout).

Many people come in to share stories about their grandmother's home remedy. Others come in just because they want to see a human or kind face.

Some who ask questions take assiduous notes and go home to think about what next steps they might want to take. We encourage people to do their own due diligence. That makes us happy. Of course, we also need people to shop so we can pay bills and keep our doors open. Yes, we want our shoppers to buy their fish oil, ashwagandha, onions, kefir, ice cream, sardines with bones, apples and their hand soap and halvah from us. We need this if we are to stay in business!

Imagine, then, a young woman who conversed with one of our staff in the supplement department for a good 40 minutes. She said how grateful she was, that now she had a plan of action. Thanked us again, profusely. Headed toward the door. Called back "Now I know exactly what to get on Amazon!"

"You know, we have that stuff, too," one of us said.

"Oh, good to know!" she said as she dashed out.

This story Adam emailed me had me laughing out loud.

> Customer comes in, a self-styled Guru of some ancient discipline or another. Whatever. He deigns to grace our establishment with his presence maybe two-three times a year, mostly so he can educate me. Bear in mind, I have never asked him to educate me. So, he comes in, and uses a manufacturer's coupon for a free loaf of bread. Doesn't buy anything, just gets that free loaf. And about a dozen samples of Zyflamend and elderberry pills, and fish oil, and wheatgrass juice concentrate, and progesterone cream. He helps himself to these samples, pretty much anything we have at the register. He reflects on the (free)

Zyflamend, says "Yes, I believe this will be acceptable." Takes another.

He then whips out a discount card. Asks what he needs to do to get the card punched. I say, "Spend $10." He asks, "How much was the bread?" I say "$4.79, although, of course, in this case it was actually free." Discussion ensues as to the nature of coupon as "payment." He tries to convince me that I do not fully understand our store policy. He sits down at the carrot table to eat a few slices. I drift back to the supplement department. The register bell rings, and I head back up. There he is: he pronounces the bread "too dry to eat." (I'm thinking: then where did those slices go?) He asks for his coupon back. Then he asks if he can leave some business cards at the cash register.

Barb (not her real name) drove us crazy for years and years with creative shenanigans, until one day we fired her as a customer. Here's the example I shared with her: on a Friday evening, she bought six or seven bottles of supplements. The next day, on a Saturday, she returned to the store with Friday's receipt and six or seven bottles to return. That would have been fine except the bottles she brought back to us on Saturday were years old and expired. And purchased at Whole Foods.

More recently she demanded her money back for multiple containers of food from our kitchen, one of which she had just eaten at our carrot table. "Disgusting," she said with contempt. Another she stated had onions (yes it did, the ingredient label listed onions), and she said, triumphantly, "I'm allergic to onions." She claimed we had changed the recipe. We hadn't.

Barb wrote that she loves our store and is desolate she isn't welcome anymore. "Where will I go?" she asked. "I promised my friend who is coming to visit from Japan that we'd go to your store and buy dinner. I told her about the carrot table," she said mournfully. "And who in their right mind would attempt a switcheroo like that with supplements?" she concluded. I told her that I agree, I also would find it unbelievable were it not for the fact that I'm the one who was asked to handle those returns on Saturday morning!

And then there is the gentleman (note that I am using the word "gentleman" loosely), who is a well-known speaker and author of books on meditation. A sister store in the Boston area once chased him on the sidewalk after witnessing him taking products and walking out. When asked "How could a man who teaches spirituality do such a thing?" he replied, "Well, no one's perfect."

He was a customer in our shop as well.

Some of you may remember the arpilleras, those vividly colored 3-D hand-stitched quilts, that hung in our store's back hallway and in the bathroom and on the bathroom door. They were large, museum-quality, made in Peru by women who shared visions of lush gardens, the undersea world, festive weddings, mountain villages. Each quilt had a pocket on the back with a note from the artist herself.

The mountain village arpillera hung in the back hallway. There were red-roofed homes hanging from the side of the mountain, goats leaping, apple orchards, children walking to school and people tilling gardens. The undersea extravaganza hung in the bathroom, and another ocean scene on the bathroom door, made it a place where people stopped to take it all in. Children asked to use the bathroom just to see the quilt with glittery fish. Waving seaweed. Squid and bright ocean flowers.

To this day, I don't know who just flicked each from the wall, rolled them up and walked out the back door. A man was seen walking with them under his arm in our back parking lot. A police sketch was drawn. The people interviewed each thought he'd purchased them. Which makes perfect sense, because 99.9 percent of the people who are guests in our store are, like we are, trusting. They are kind souls.

There was an outpouring of grief about our arpilleras. People mourned that they'd no longer be able to touch the baskets of fruit or finny creatures swimming under the sea.

Every few years we conduct a customer survey and ask our peeps to tell us what they think of us. Their answers also tell us who they are. I summarize the findings and report back to staff. Our last survey garnered some of these responses.

"I feel like I am coming home when I shop here." "I would love for you to be bigger, but please don't ever leave W. Concord. You are a major factor in my loving living here." You're our favorite place in Concord!" "You guys rock! Don't ever go away." "I moved away for a year and Debra's was what I missed most. I went to four stores carrying natural and organic products and still couldn't get everything I wanted!"

"Love the soups, greens and treats, in that order." "Smells great when I walk in the door." "Grace's hugs!" "Music, of course!" "The atmosphere, friendliness, great products!" "Light and bright, energetically as well as visually." "Community-orient-ed; committed to the best!" "Organic produce, knowledgeable staff." "I thought I'd say that my favorite in your store are the prepared foods, but I can't since I love everything!" "I LOVE the bulk herbs and spices." "Health and beauty section." "Deb-ra's is not just a store, it's a huge part of the community." "Sense of fidelity to ethics."

"This place is better known than you think. I was in Ontario with one of your purple bags, and they knew about this place!" "I was coming down an escalator in San Francisco with one or your purple bags and someone coming up the elevator passed me and held up his purple Debra's bag!"

One new customer took the time to email me:

"This may sound silly, but I was completely stressed about my work assignment in Concord, because of the way I eat. I packed a Nutribullet and many powdered greens. I live in NYC and I thought I had access to everything. I was wrong! Your store is the real thing. I met Brendon (B) in your store and explained my relief (which might sound crazy). He introduced me to your raw, organic vegetable juices, and I drank three a day when I was there (and came home and tried to replicate your recipes). B was a delight and introduced me to Cado Ice Cream, the seed chips and many other treasures.

"Thank you for the time, energy and effort into creating some-thing so authentic, real and made with care/love. It is apparent and I sincerely appreciate it. Warmly, Francesca"

We are a mutual admiration society. We admire our customers right back and pray that they will multiply like rabbits. But there was one disgruntled fellow, whom none of us recognized, stalking through the store, glowering. Finally, he sought me out. "You the owner?" he challenged. "You're all sickening." He finished with a verbal flourish of the sword, "People in health food stores are crap. They're sickly because of this organic stuff. You all look too damn healthy. What's wrong with you all, anyway?" And he stalked out. Never to be seen again.

I think he would have appreciated this joke by Redd Foxx. "Health nuts are going to feel stupid someday, lying in hospitals dying of nothing."

Chapter 7

Staff Through The Years

I'll always love what Adam put on Facebook in January of 2017.

> This Monday, almost two dozen members of the DNG family are scheduled to work. We'll meet the early deliveries, open the doors, stock the shelves, chop and cook, help you find what you're looking for and show you to the door with a smile. If you've shopped here before, you probably recognize some of us.
>
> Most of us are US citizens by birth. But among us this Monday will be more than one immigrant, and two legal permanent residents awaiting citizenship. One of us came to the US as a child refugee, and at least one of us has a spouse with a green card. Wherever we came from, and however we got here, we'll spend the day together. At the end of the day, we will return to the neighborhoods we share, as each other's neighbors and friends.
>
> Without any one of us, we wouldn't be the same. We couldn't imagine it any other way.

In the early days, when there were only six employees, I made fresh vegetable juice and lentil soup for our whole team. Now that there are 57 staffers, all of whom work different hours and different shifts, and now that I am no longer in the kitchen, and not even in the store every day, juice and soup is off the table.

That isn't to say that we're no longer a team. We are. We have each other's backs. And when we interview applicants to join our shop, we look for folks who want to be a part of our community. I define our community as a group of people who laugh at the same stuff–which is an oversimplification, I know. As Gary Erickson of the company Clif Bar says, because there's an "intimacy with customers that is intensely and unexpectedly personal," we need people who can listen and share stories, both.

As for sharing stories, I mean staff who can tell stories about the people who sell us eggs, the farmer who uses his fall raspberries to make raspberry vinegar, our industry which grapples with issues around Fair Trade and fair labor, and soil health.

There's a lot of history about how we came to be and why each of us, individually, is here in the shop. A Native American proverb says, "It takes a thousand voices to tell a single story." Our staff do that and are our brand. And I love that our brand is not homogeneous but has nooks and crannies.

Like with every crowd, over more than a quarter of a century, our staff has had its characters. One gent left us to become a bug exterminator (we refer to him as the "bug man") and another sits in federal prison for robbing a bank in Colorado. It makes a good story, but I try not to think about his mother or father because I know this is more than just a story to them. I can't imagine their sorrow. Nor was it funny when he smashed into our store and fled westward ho with thousands of dollars.

We had a former staffer say up at the register, "Yeah, that'll cure cancer." Yes, it takes all kinds. Our staff has had the usual suspects: nutcases, alcoholics, a staffer who raided our shelves in the middle of the night (he had a store key) to bring home more pizza and Q-Tonic for a shin-dig already in full swing. We've had more than one employee change sexual orientation while they were with us. One of these announced his switcheroo by suddenly adopting the style of loafers sans socks and getting an ear pierced.

We've dealt with mental illness. We're no stranger to sexual harassment. We had one disgruntled staffer tell Goldie Hawn when she was in our store that just because she looked like Goldie Hawn was no reason to act like her! We had a brother and sister who worked with a gang of thieves.

We are part of the work release program at the prison, and we've had veterans. One of our vets, who worked in the kitchen, would have upped and left us without notice had he not bumped into Mary Kadlik (who was then our kitchen manager) in the parking lot. "I'm a man of God now," Joseph said. "I'm leaving with my flock in the morning for Florida." Before he left, we briefly had Mary, Joseph and Jesus chop-ping side by side.

Speaking of the kitchen, we've had dueling knives there, but that's a thing of the past, and our kitchen is one of the happiest places in the whole store. Neither combatant is still with us, but suffice it to say that we hear they're both doing fine.

Now if only we could get a 5:00 a.m. juicer, Roxanne and Casey and Cassandra could sleep in a little. (After I wrote this, we had to cut juicing down to one day a week or kill our kitchen staff. The hunt is on to hire a terrific early morning juicer we hope will stay with us forever.)

Speaking of our kitchen, when cooks joined me, they found that I had no written recipes. I cavalierly assumed anyone would follow along, follow my lead by osmosis. My split pea soup would be their split pea soup. It was Mary Kadlik, with whom I've worked longer than with anyone else, who sat me in front of the computer and forced me to put everything in writing. Voilà! Our first cookbook was born in 1991.

Speaking of folks who've worked in our kitchen, I once wrote the following: "Dear R–following recipes is like playing a piece of music. You play the notes as written, and when you play a wrong note, you don't say, 'Next time I'll leave out the last measure!'

"The amount of salt or cinnamon or curry powder is written down because that's the amount that makes the dish sing. That's the amount you have to use, exactly. Our customers expect consistency. Following a recipe in our kitchen doesn't give you leave to improvise! Just like playing Beethoven's 5th can't be improvised."

Today, our cooks follow house recipes. Most are the original recipes from the early years. They live in our three cookbooks. Some have been "improved"–the kitchen now roasts chicken for Mom's Chicken Barley Soup, whereas I used to dice it and just throw it into the soup kettle together with everything else. Some of our best-selling recipes today are either new and improved or brand new. Maybe someday there will be a fourth cookbook.

Over the years we've had three farmers sign on for wintertime work at Debra's. Elena Colman said that she always appreciated being able to keep her feet warm and dry with us when she couldn't be in the fields. Ray Mong (the Mong family farms Applefield Farm in Stow, MA) has been with us many years, and we are his farm's largest customer in the summer. You should see the glorious produce we get!

We had one charming fellow with an accent (swoon), soft voice and bright blue eyes. It was our misfortune that both his dog and daughter had favorite products in our store, which disappeared out the back door. And after we scooted *him* out the same door, his "patients" profusely thanked us, said how kind we were to allow him to sell our Debra's brand supplements. Apparently, he'd been waltzing out with full cases, along with dog food and face cream, for months before we let him go. Sure, we were dopes. But is trusting people a bad thing? There are so few bad apples.

One person who emailed me about a job opening said that the smell of fresh baked goods always had a calming effect on his volatile temper. I think that may have been a joke, but just in case, we didn't bring him in for an interview.

I did hire a sweet young man who dressed all in black (we've had several gentlemen who wore nothing but black over the years). This young man was a stocker, but he wouldn't come out of the basement. To give him credit, the music he played down there was extraordinary. And the basement was neater, cleaner and more beautifully arranged than the shop upstairs.

I saw nothing wrong with this picture until my friend, Rick Antonelli, formerly prez of our major distributor, visited and pointed out that we had no customers shopping in the basement. We didn't need a second shop downstairs. Inventory belonged upstairs, Rick said.

Our young man left soon after because he couldn't face the world upstairs.

I like to think we've gotten hiring *down* after 30 years. Our staff are extraordinary. That includes our teenagers and college kids who, no matter their age, pull their own weight. A couple of parents have thanked us for teaching their kids responsibility. One parent said they not only made out like bandits with the family staff discount, but no longer needed to pay a psychologist because we were so much more effective. Another father said he was amazed that after working with us, nes gadol hayah sham (Hebrew for "a big miracle was there"), his son could clean a bathroom.

In our kitchen, Roxanne and the rest of the adult crew are grateful that our young people massage kale, get lickety-split fast at peeling hard-boiled eggs (many dozens a day!) and wrap cookies. They weigh organic frozen fruit ahead of time for smoothies and scrub the pans from baking muffins. We can't do without these young people. Brandon relishes their help with pots and pans, too.

Elsewhere in the store, our kids, as we call them, help our shoppers, bag lettuce, run the registers, find missing cases of tomato sauce and clean the parking lot.

When our young 'uns go off to college and come back on breaks and school vacations, it's not only a Godsend, but pure pleasure. Watching them interact with our new batch of high school ducklings, who are still getting their feet wet, is great fun.

On the other end of the age spectrum, I remember when the guys at Phillips Hardware said how kind I was to hire a senior citizen. From across the street and through their window and into ours, they were watching my mom, then in her late 70s, lift 25-pound bags of parsnips.

But then, as now, we have an outstanding crew over the age of 70 and 80, and we all lift and carry. No one can put stuff away faster and so neatly as Mary. She talks to people about reversing bone loss as well, based on her own experience. No one catches expired products better than MaryJane, who also keeps the herb and spice bins full. No one dispenses hugs and commonsense like Grace. Downstairs, Barbara pays our bills and Gail (a young damsel, but mentioned here because Gail and Barbara are a dynamic duo) enters products into our point of sale system. Upstairs again, no one networks better than Pat. No one gets the numbers and carries them around in his head better than Jim (who is still a young shaver in his 60s). Jim also writes a poem for our annual staff party each year in which he manages to fit the name of every single staff person. I'd share, except you've got to be on staff to get all the inside jokes.

The majority of our crew are neither young, nor the AARP crowd, and are the next gen. I'm speaking of Adam, David Abbott, Roxanne Bispham, Alexander Gardner, Meg Stone and more.

Our staff are lovable characters. Pat used to manage environmental projects around the world. She is a mover and shaker in the community. Retired, she plays tennis and keeps us all on our toes. She was heard exclaiming to a customer buying pluots (a pluot is mostly plum with some apricot mixed in) that she'd never seen anything whose skin looked so pathological.

Jay, back in supplements, who also guides a meditation group in the store, told me he could barely keep a straight face when he heard Grace (Grace, to be fair, is a nurse) tell a customer with IBS that the customer had to watch her milk consumption because it would affect her in the "dairy area." Alexander, who started in the store as a teenager (he's now in college), suffers from many allergies. As a high schooler, he tried eating hemp seeds, but had an allergic reaction. "At least you won't have to worry about my smoking weed," he said to his mom, Roxanne.

Our staff can be hilarious. An example of that is when I challenged everyone to come up with a new way to market our store. The winning scheme, and this goes back 20 years, was a singles' shopping night. Which lead to imagining the best pickup lines for singles shopping in a natural products store. The winner was, "So, do you buy colon cleansers often?"

Because we are many and I want us all to be on the same page, I write a staff memo, which gets attached to paychecks. And every couple of years I ask everyone to write something about themselves that the rest of us might not know. I am sharing some snippets because they give you a sense of who our staff are, and because some of their stories made me laugh out loud.

Alex: Some folks may know, but I've loved the beauty of fields and fences all my life. I have certain landscapes lodged in my memory that I still paint today. I enjoy painting the fields, and more than anything, a random colorful sky to fit my mood.

Casey: I always wanted to be a dentist.

Charles: I once worked as an apprentice at the fine art sculpture foundry of Seward Johnson, one of the Johnson & Johnson heirs. Johnson liked to create life sized figures of people engaged in ordinary activities that were then displayed in public spaces. His intention was to create art that ordinary people would identify with and relate to.

Sometimes we did casting for other famous artists. One of my favorite projects was working on a sculpture of Georgia O'Keeffe based on her painting "Ram's Horn."

Cheryl: I bought a pair of feeder goldfish and one of them lived to be 13 years old. His name was Danny. He was 3/8" long when I bought him and his pal for 14 cents. He grew and grew, and I kept upgrading his aquarium. I had to move to a bigger apartment to accommodate his 50-gallon tank! Danny jumped around happily when I walked up to his aquarium.

In addition, when Danny was very young (and tiny) he was all white with a little orange round spot on the top of his head. My friend Daniel (a nice Jewish boy) after whom Danny was named, told me that the fish was clearly Jewish as he was born wearing a Yarmulke. All Danny's life we looked forward to his turning 13 so we could celebrate his Bar Mitzvah. Daniel and I grieved over Danny's passing in 2009, two months after his Bar Mitzvah. We still miss him. He was an amazing little being and a very good friend.

Dave: When I was in ninth grade, my friend and I created a short movie for a filmmaking class ("Burgled Hams") in which I ran around West Concord wearing a Hamburglar costume, stealing sandwiches, getting chased, etc. Several of the shots were right around the sidewalk and parking lot of DNG, so one can just imagine that on some rainy Saturday in 2001, Debra could have looked out the window and seen me running around dressed as a ridiculous fast food character!

David: I have a college degree in Criminal Justice. I was accepted to multiple Boston law schools but never attended.

Gail: A friend said, "You have more rocks in your house than Ogunquit has sand." To my chagrin, I realized that he was right. Not only do I have a large stash of stones for jewelry making, each room has rocks on display and pictures of stones on the walls, there is a hunk of marble in the trunk of my car and I even spent several months gluing approximately 15,000 pebbles and glass tiles to a wall in my living room.

Grace: My first job as an RN was the night shift in the delivery room at Leonard Moss Hospital in Natick. I was the only nurse on that shift for two years! I learned how to deliver babies very fast.

Gregoria: When I was growing up, I played a lot of soccer. I was pretty good! I have just started playing again.

Hilton: In November 1991 traveling in Canada, fueled by the enthusiasm and overconfidence that was indicative of my young self, I decided to make an impromptu solo attempt to reach the North Pole! I took transport to an Inuit village 500 kilometers from the North Pole. I believed that if I spent ten days with indigenous people first, I would learn all there was to learn about survival in the Arctic. I procured transport, which it turned out could not even reach my destination. Still, I packed up, dismissed cautions about polar bears and needing a firearm, and gaily headed forth. After three days, standing outside my tent looking at the Northern Lights, my eyeballs started to freeze behind my ski glasses. (Ask me about this!) I swallowed my pride, headed back the same way I'd come, thanked everyone for their advice, paid for the transport, and here I am today to tell the tale.

Jay: Prince sent his bodyguards after me because I had the "audacity" to watch him do his soundcheck before a concert. My office was in the concert hall that he was performing in and when I heard him start to play, I went to take a peek.

Jim: My great grandmother used to make bullets for the Fenians (the precursors to the IRA) in the late nineteenth century.

On Father's Day 30 years ago, I ran up Mount Washington. They hold an annual race up the auto road. It was a 7.6-mile race, but there was only one hill!

Mary: I can tell you about any one of my nine grandchildren or I can tell you about the many neighborhood parties we had that were raided by the police, once with police dogs. Just ask Mary.

Meg: For the past decade, before coming to Debra's, I worked, volunteered and interned in animal care. Some of my favorite and most memorable charges include northern fur seals, red foxes, a porcupine, bald eagles, bottle-nosed dolphins, turkey vulture, red shoulder hawk and a black and white regu named Pablo.

Mitch: In 2001 I was the mascot at UMass Amherst. Hmmm, well, it entailed going to cheerleading practices. My buddies thought this was awesome, but in reality, the cheerleaders do not speak to the mascots. The scariest thing was running on to the football field in the costume, with the football team right behind you, before games.

Nathan: In 2009, I volunteered to help an energy healer practice her craft. I had a beautifully positive experience; however, my reaction was so intense that I yelled and spasmed for a week straight...So, there's that.

Pat: From working as a picker in the apricot orchards in California to working as a movie extra in Rome, I am thrilled to now be at Debra's Natural Gourmet. Dare I confess that the movies included Perversion

Story and Untouchables? Apricot picking was HARD work but great for an eastern kid who had NO idea of farm labor.

Paul: I am very much into studying the fascinating subjects of astronomy, outer space and the universe. I am also on a record label with wonderful musicians from all over the world!

Rakhi: My passion is cooking and reading books. I love to care for my family and other people in my life. I like to be strong in any situations.

Rebecca: I've picked and pressed Zeitoun (olives) in Palestine and spent time in Israel, too.

Robin: My grandfather was the captain of the Albatross IV, a NOAA Fishing vessel. When I was a little girl in the early seventies, we were invited aboard a Russian vessel that was in dry dock at Woods Hole. It was during the Cold War era and I was so terrified that I initially refused to go, fearing something very bad would happen to both myself and my family. I believed, then, that the Russians were very bad and would cause harm to our country. The meeting was scary at first, but the Russian Captain presented me with a Matryoshka doll, and the adults were given Stolichnaya and Beluga Caviar. I remember the adults and the Russians toasting with the vodka. I do have memories that the Russian Captain was very kind to me. My mom remembers me speaking with a Russian crew member in English, he was talking to me in Russian and she said we were both smiling and communicating without even understanding each other. She said she could feel the camaraderie.

Roxanne: I grew up in a small town with population of less than a thousand people in Connecticut. My graduating eighth grade class was 16 kids! We had all been together since kindergarten. Since we didn't have a high school, we were bused to a surrounding town 45 minutes away. We had no police, the post office was in a house, and our fire department/emergency services was made up of volunteers who lived in the town. We had a milk man until I went to college, an egg man who delivered once a week and a Finnish bread man who sold his freshly baked bread out the back of this station wagon. I'm a country mouse who moved to Massachusetts and became a city mouse!

Tori: When I was 12, I decided I wanted to work in the food industry because of Melissa McCarthy's character, Sookie, on the TV show Gilmore Girls.

Vivian (Vivian was our beloved accountant for 28 years): When I graduated college, public accounting firms were not hiring women. When I went for interviews, I went in masquerade; I wore a three-piece suit, my hair in a bun and borrowed glasses that probably made me legally blind! When I showed up for my first day on the job in a flowery summer dress, sans bun, sans glasses, the interviewers hardly recognized me! Three years later they were sending me out to college campuses to do the interviewing–times had changed!

Wendy: I love my time doing music therapy with special needs and medically fragile children. I've learned that no matter what someone's disability, people need to be accepted as they are and loved.

Because we love our staff and wouldn't be anywhere without them, we share profits. Some staffers use their extra $ for yoga or joining the Beede Center. One person used hers to buy a bed for her guest room, and another paid for a night class to study Arabic.

A former staffer wrote this thank you note: "Debra, as you know I worked at Fidelity for ten years. In that ten years I received one Holiday bonus of $1000, which was a big deal and pretty much without precedent. If you take that and divide by ten it was $100 a year. The Johnson family (owners of Fidelity) had at that time roughly three trillion in assets under management, and a small company of 70 people managing their wealth. If you worked backwards given the store's net worth, the gift you gave me was at least a thousand times greater than what was given to me by a multi-billionaire. I've worked at Debra's under a year, so your gift is even greater than the Johnson family's."

Our staff hold it together when the tractor trailer arrives in the wee hours with the order for a store in Pennsylvania. We pull together when someone falls. When a freezer goes on the fritz and the ice cream needs to be saved, we carry on. When a register stops working, when all the lights go out in a storm, our staff figures something out.

In a 2009 staff memo, I wrote that I was amazed how well we all work together and at how hard everyone works. Jim pointed out that each Wednesday's early morning delivery is about 5,000 pounds of all kinds of food and products that get opened and put onto shelves, into bins and into refrigerators and freezers, most of it before the store opens. That's a lot of stuff. I am proud of the teamwork that makes this look so easy. No matter what's going on behind the scenes, our staff have become adept at standup comedy and impromptu theater.

My job the days I'm in the shop is to drive everyone crazy. I challenge everyone to keep learning about organic farming and food ingredients. I encourage everyone to vote. To take their vitamin D. I challenge our staff to learn to play the game of business. I want them to notice things like the tails on the plastic bags that hold breads. Are they neatly facing in or sloppily facing out on the shelves? They roll their eyes, and sometimes they humor me. But I want our staff to "Cherylize" the store. Cheryl has such a good eye for design that when she touches the cheeses or anything else in the store, she makes them look like a work of art.

And I know how lucky we are to have others who also see things through an artist's eyes. Meg's been doing our windows. I've never seen anyone with such gorgeous handwriting as Rebecca. Back in the kitchen, Cassandra is an artist and Tory has quite the touch piping onto baked goods.

But I digress. We know that it's our staff's passion that people remember. It's courtesy, Emily's good humor, the repartee between Andrew and B and Wendy's kindness that make our customers come back. We know tone of voice really does matter, and that everyone feels better when greeted with a smile. That's what our staff do so well.

Chapter 8

Our Companies

My brother David sent me this from The Associated Press:

> It's rare to find kosher ham. Rarer still to find it carbonated and bottled. Jones Soda Co., the Seattle-based purveyor of offbeat fizzy water, said Friday that it was shelving its traditional seasonal flavors of turkey and gravy this year to produce limited-edition theme packs for Christmas and Hanukkah.
>
> The Christmas pack will feature such flavors as Sugar Plum, Christmas Tree, Eggnog and Christmas Ham. The Hanukkah pack will have Jelly Doughnut, Apple Sauce, Chocolate Coins and Latkes sodas. "As always, both packs are kosher and contain zero caffeine," a Jones news release noted.

This is a hoot. Jones Sodas are witty and they're fun. They pride themselves on using pure cane sugar. On the other hand, pure cane sugar isn't something to beat the band about, especially when you consider the other ingredients in their sodas like artificial flavors, phosphoric acid, the preservatives sodium benzoate and potassium sorbate, and calcium disodium EDTA, which, they say, protects flavor.

Calcium disodium EDTA *is* widely used in the US in our foods, but unfortunately it can have adverse effects such as nausea, muscle weakness, headache, dizziness, and heart palpitations. According to the US Food and Drug Administration, eleven people died from exposure to calcium disodium EDTA between 1971 and 2007. That's not even one person a year, but I'd still prefer to skip EDTA.

Because of these ingredients, you can't buy Jones Sodas in our store. Nor can you find Hostess Ding Dongs with their 32 ingredients such as Mono- and Diglycerides, Polysorbate 60. You won't find Reddi Whip with its corn syrup and nitrous oxide as propellant.

Our distributors don't carry these or so many other "foods" considered fine and dandy in the US. These are not our companies. You won't find them at our trade shows or on our shelves.

All this is not to say that we, our companies and the natural products industry are angels. We have our rogue players, and we have a lot of products with cane sugar. A historical note here—sugar cane and all refined sweeteners were verboten in our world until Whole Foods changed standards and said, "Bring it on!" The floodgates then opened because sugar is easier to work with, easier to source, and it's much cheaper than honey, maple syrup or coconut sugar (which is a whole different animal).

We had no choice but to change some of our standards when products we loved disappeared, and when our choices of new products in categories, like ice cream for instance, became slim. If you wanted to sell ice cream, you had to bring in the ones that now marched to the drummer inspired by Whole Foods.

But our companies are all over the map, both literally and figuratively. They're farmers who grow kamut and brown rice. They're disrupters who decide cauliflower would make a fine pizza crust. They're Beyond Meat, whose stock went up more than 500 percent in one day in 2019. Our companies both set trends and bring back foods our grandmothers loved. They introduce us to ingredients from around the world.

Remember when we first learned about quinoa, an ancient grain grown in Peru? Remember when we couldn't pronounce it? Keen-OH-ah, people would say. But one of our companies, Ancient Harvest, was passionate and brought quinoa to market. In addition to the whole grain, they brought us quinoa pasta. Who wudda thunk?

We count among our tribe explorers who make friends in Vanuatu and Sri Lanka and the rainforests of Brazil. They form partnerships that benefit everyone and that strengthen diversity of culture and plants.

Think about jack fruit. Monk fruit. Goji berries and camu camu. About fermented beets, heirloom seeds from around the world, Himalayan salt and black garlic.

Our supplement companies research ancient traditions via modern science and introduce us to neem, astaxanthin and black seed oil. Our health and beauty companies bring us healing salves that combine folk medicine with newfangled standardization.

Meg Stone, our health and beauty department manager, asks if you've tried Bee Magic for rashes and everything skin related. She goes gaga over lotions and potions that not only make skin glow, but have been created by companies whose missions resonate. And who don't hurt animals.

We have brands that satisfy vegans, meat lovers, the dairy and no-dairy crowds. The just-fantastic-all-kinds-of-foods crowd. Our companies work hard to attain organic certification, biodynamic status, the Non-GMO logo and many other verifications.

When I go out into the greater world, even when I have dinner with friends, I feel sometimes as if I live in a bubble. The world outside my own kitchen and outside our industry can feel alien. Take this example of a company we can't believe really exists–Adam sent me this email in 2009:

> I couldn't make this stuff up. There's a new product on the market that can change your life, make you feel better, live longer, etc., etc., etc...It's a cholesterol-lowering...suppository! Yes, suppository. Just Google 'Medicardium'–you'll learn all about it. (I love the fact that the first hit on the search engine talks about using it "in the comfort of your own home." As opposed to what–on the bus?)

Unlike the company that makes Medicardium, most of our companies are our heroes. I feel the need to name some here so you can fall in love with them, too, though I run the risk of hurting feelings because there are so many who deserve mention and our thanks.

Now, drum roll, please! I laugh at myself that my first company is an ice cream company, but Three Twins Ice Cream is an example of a company that works to improve our world. Neal H. Gottlieb, Three

Twins Ice Cream founder, traveled to the wilds of Cambodia to be a contestant on the television program "Survivor." (He didn't win but left with a staph infection on his leg.) Among many good deeds Neal has done, he started *Ice Cream for Acres*. To save land for humanity, as it were. Every package carries the logo of Earth in an ice cream cone, and a statement of how much land Three Twins will buy because of the purchase. An individual sundae cone buys two square feet, a pint six square feet, and a quart, ten square feet. Some ten years ago, Three Twins consumers had already purchased 8,000 acres.

Ken Lee and Caryl Levine, husband and wife, took a meandering path to co-founding Lotus Foods in 1995. In 1993 they took a two-month research trip to China. They discovered heirloom black rice in Yunnan province and were intrigued by its flavor, health benefits and ancient history (it was offered to the emperors as a symbol of longevity). On the spot, they saw their future as selling specialty varieties of rice to support biodiversity around the planet. They won over local chefs in San Francisco, and soon they were able to connect small rice farmers to a distribution channel. They wrestled higher premiums for their farmers. But what is so impressive about Lee and Levine is that they pioneered a different way to grow rice. Their campaign to educate people is called *More Crop Per Drop*. Their tag line is "Water Smart, Women Strong, and Climate Wise."

Most of us think of rice as an aquatic plant, growing in fields of water. Yet rice does not require the traditional method of flooding fields, which wastes humongous amounts of water. Flooding fields also diminishes soil health, contributes to global warming by emitting methane gas (which has 30 times the warming effect of carbon dioxide).

And working in flooded fields impacts the health of women, because women are the ones who work the fields, by never letting their feet dry.

Lee and Levine's methods have nearly tripled family incomes and doubled, sometimes tripled rice yields. It has cut methane emissions, uses 50 percent less water. 528 million gallons of water were saved in 2015, and today Lotus Foods works with 4,000 small producers around the globe.

We're proud to sell bakery products from Little Stream Bakery in Ontario, Canada. Why go so far afield for bread? Adam says that Little Stream is environmentally close to perfect, in too many ways to mention. They grind their own grains. They use well water. Their loaves, both spelt and gluten-free, are dense and thick. (You want an airy, chewy loaf? Little Stream ain't for you). Their spelt-hemp loaf is full of protein and omega-3s from the hemp seeds. I love their spelt-hemp bread (it rocks!) but am not a fan of their buckwheat (gluten-free) bread. Gag. That's why there is vanilla and chocolate ice cream.

David Abbott, who wears many management hats, came to us from Stop & Shop supermarkets, and, boy, has he caught fire in our store. He does a lot of buying for our shop. Three of his fave companies, he says, are Equal Exchange, Walden Local Meat and Garden Spot Distributors.

"Equal Exchange promotes fair-trade certification to the point that until I visited their headquarters in Bridgewater, MA, I actually thought they were a non-profit organization. According to them I am not the only one who is under this impression! They are one of a handful of companies we choose to deal with directly, instead of through distributors, just so we can maintain our friendship and personal relationship. Equal Exchange owners have been known to make emergency hand-deliveries.

"Walden Local Meat really sticks to their roots, occasionally to my chagrin, but they always have my respect. They started as a home delivery service, and even though they have since added wholesale and their own retail butcher shop, they honor those first customers. I am constantly begging them for products I see on their website, but unless they have enough for their home delivery members, they say no. Yes, it drives me crazy, but I understand their reasoning. Our shoppers comment that they know they can trust us because we carry Walden meats.

"Garden Spot Distributors. We sell thousands of product lines and dealing with thousands of companies is logistically impossible. Garden Spot is a small distributor with eclectic groceries, and I'm happy to say I have the email address for their head of procurement. He's been a great partner taking recommendations and allowing me to play matchmaker for little companies we found like Happy Campers bread, Yoot teas, and UpRise Foods Nooch It vegan cashew cheese. A win-win for Garden Spot, the little companies starting out, and for us."

Adam found Brooklyn Delhi, a company located, gasp, in Brooklyn. Their tomato aachar sauce won a Sofi at the Fancy Food Show (not to mention a Good Food Award, The Front Burner Competition and a FABI). Chitra, the founder of the company, says she would never use preservatives like citric or lactic acid, stabilizers like xanthan or guar gum, or starches like corn or tapioca. She uses the same ingredients she uses in her home kitchen. And that's why Madhur Jaffrey, the award-winning cookbook author, said, *"I loved Brooklyn Delhi's tomato achaar so much!"*

Real Pickles is one of our local, organic companies. In 2019 their organic garlic dills and organic garlic kraut received the Good Food Awards, which "recognizes American food and drink crafters who create tasty, authentic and responsible products and, in doing so, better the nation's food system." Real Pickles co-owners Kristin Howard and Katie Korby were congratulated by renowned chef Alice Waters and Slow Food founder Carlo Petrini, who handed them their awards.

Also local are Mi Tierra Tortillas. Mi Tierra grows their own corn and delivers their made-in-Massachusetts organic tortillas to us weekly.

We love our local honeys, and our honeys from Canada and Hawaii, all of whom worry about our bees. We love Butternut Mountain maple syrup that we've been carrying since 1990, and Mansfield Maple, Mount Cabot and Hidden Springs maple syrups we've added since then.

Speaking of a company on a mission, Sindyanna of Galilee, Israel, is a non-profit organization which "facilitates a partnership between Jewish and Arab women and Arab farmers by combining commercial activity and community programs and peace building." They have several olive oil labels, and currently we've chosen to shelve the one carried by Serrv, a non-profit organization which carries products from around the world. Anytime you buy a Serrv product, you know you done good!

We have so many stellar olive oil companies, but Holy Smoke smokes theirs and says right on the bottle that smoking makes it taste just like bacon. It does! Here's recipe to try:

Asparagus Parsnip Soup with Smoked Olive Oil

This soup is light, light, light, but the parsnip gives body, and together with the asparagus and celery yields a lovely, complex flavor.

Makes 4-6 servings

2 bunches asparagus, about 2¼ lbs	1 Tbsp good salt
3 Tbsp smoked EVOO	1 tsp ground black pepper
2 yellow onions, chopped (3 C)	1 Tbsp fresh dill weed,
4 cloves garlic, minced	or 2 tsp dried
½ C diced celery	3 more Tbsp smoked EVOO oil
1 C minced parsnip	more dill as garnish
6 C water	1 Tbsp lemon juice, optional

In a soup pot, gently warm smoked olive oil. Add onions, garlic, celery and parsnip. Sauté until onions are soft and translucent, about 10 minutes. Stir from time to time. In the meantime, cut the tips off of the asparagus spears and set aside. Cut the remaining spears into 1-inch pieces. Add the asparagus pieces to the pot, along with the water, salt, pepper and dill. Bring gently to a boil, turn heat to low, cover pot and simmer about 10 minutes, until vegetables are tender.

Using another small pot, bring a cup of water to a boil. Add reserved asparagus tips and simmer a few minutes until tender-crisp. Drain and refresh under cold water or in an ice bath. Set aside. (Our kitchen tosses the tips with more smoked olive oil and roasts them in a 350-degree oven. I don't take the time.)

Purée the soup with a blender or a food processor (my Vitamix renders this velvety in a few seconds). You'll need, of course, to blend in two or three batches so your machine doesn't flow over with soup! As you blend, return each batch to a new, waiting pot. Bring soup back to a simmer. Stir in the additional smoked olive oil. Taste and adjust seasonings, add lemon juice if you like. Ladle soup into bowls, then top each bowl with the reserved asparagus tips, more dill and another grinding of pepper.

• •

We adore the whole sesame tahini brought to us by Oxygen Imports, from Israel, and their date syrup, too. Whole sesame tahini is hard to find but so worth it for the magnesium in its unhulled sesame seeds.

We love all the Eden Food Products, which are first rate and do right by all their farmers. Eden beans are the only beans cooked with kombu, a piece of seaweed that helps with digestibility and minimizes discomfort people can experience when they eat beans. (Beans, beans, that musical fruit. Not with Eden Beans, and that's why we use Eden beans in our kitchen.)

I go nuts over Rise Matcha Mint CBD Morsels, which is my bedtime treat. They melt in your mouth. Oh, my goodness.

Adam brought us Sophia's Yogurt. Shelburne Farms sells us their cheddars from Vermont. Nettle Meadows has goat and sheep cheese divine. Our cheese selection in our small store is outrageously delicious with all kinds of small family farms who allow their animals to graze. Grass-fed dairy has higher amounts of CLA (conjugated linoleic acid) than feedlot, and CLA is said to help prevent belly fat.

Nutiva's coconut products are stellar. Manitoba Hemp has terrific hemp seeds. Nut butters come from companies large and small. They're roasted and raw. They're sprouted. They're not sprouted.

And I have to mention Global Balance (cleaning products) and Alan Benjamin and his ratty cardboard boxes. Alan delivers our orders himself in cardboard boxes that he unloads, takes back and uses over and over again until they fall apart. I have Alan's dishwashing liquid next to my sink. I also have Bi-O-Kleen non-bleach at home and Ecover stain remover. I love my Japanese laundry magnesium beads in a little pouch, that bubble when they get wet. Those magnesium beads clean your laundry for 365 washes. Talk about environmentally friendly! Terra Wash+Mg says they're saving the planet one wash at a time!

I've got a Himalayan salt lamp from the Himalayan Salt Company next to my computer and another one in my bedroom. I never turn them off and believe they release those negative ions into the air just like the salt air you breathe at the beach which makes us feel so good. I'm sure it's not as good as being at the beach, toes in the sand, but I love their soft glow.

Styrian Pumpkin Seed Oil from pumpkinseedoil.cc gets rave reviews. We order this dark green oil, which is a gold award-winner, directly from Austria. Our kitchen uses it to make our signature raw kale salad, which is delish because of the quality of ingredients, including, hands down, the best, most flavorful pumpkin seed oil. Austrian pumpkin seed oil, which uses hull-less pumpkin seeds from Styrian pumpkins, is made by soaking the seeds in saltwater, and then roasting them, which takes the flavor profile to a whole another level. Aromatic like there's no tomorrow. Settle for no other brand!

Now, like most of you, I didn't grow up eating kale. Left to my own devices, I'd probably choose ice cream instead. However, kale is a hardy green that is nutrient-rich and worth getting to know. The Center for Science in the Public Interest says so!

Avocados are one of my favorite foods. They have good fat that, just like the fat from pumpkin seeds, keeps our brain cells more flexible, keeps our hair shiny, and our skin silky. Don't be afraid of good fat. Studies actually show that people who eat good fats instead of going the fat-free route, have fewer problems with weight control. Amazingly, avocados also have protein and calcium!

Raw Kale Salad

Serves 4-6

1 bunch curly kale	½ C Styrian Austrian
1 tsp good salt	pumpkin seed oil
½ C sliced red onion	2 ripe Hass avocados,
1 C grated carrot, peel left on	halved, peeled, cubed
¼ C lemon or lime juice	

Shake kale under water. Shake again to remove as much water as possible. Tear kale into bite-sized pieces. I use the stems too, but most people don't because they're quite chewy. If you don't want to put the stems in your salad, save them to throw into soups, or to make vegetable stock.

Put kale in a large bowl together with salt. Massage kale for a few minutes, to tenderize.

Add onion, carrot and lemon or lime juice and pumpkin seed oil. Massage everything another minute to mix. If you can, let salad marinate an hour before adding avocado and serving to cries of joy. I most always remember to save at least half an avocado to garnish my dished-out salad plates.

• •

Elizabeth's company, Fat Moon Farms, grows mushrooms, including medicinal mushrooms that used to be rare. Thanks to her, we get to eat fresh Lion's Mane mushrooms for brain and nerve-endings. Ray and his family and the crew from Applefield Farms bring us glorious vegetables. Ray's corn is sweet and tender, and make sure to take a gander at his early onions and late summer melons.

Mary Jane orders organic bulk herbs from Frontier Herb and Spice and from Mountain Rose. Our teas come from companies on missions like Traditional Medicinals, Rishi, Divinitea, Mem tea, Yogi, Eden and Choice. Koukla's raw treats are a yummy cookie from Canada that goes great with a cuppa (one of my personal favorites).

Who hasn't heard of Dr. Bronner's? Dr. B. products are a staple in natural product stores, and Dr. Bronner's has been one of the most vocal and financially generous backers of mandatory GMO labeling. "If we don't win the right to label and enable people to choose non-GMO," CEO David Bronner told *Mother Jones*, "then everything is going to be GMO." Bronner's company is active in the legalization of hemp and marijuana, as well as preserving fair trade and organic standards.

There are skin care companies that do us proud. Weleda's diaper care cream has healed many a bum, and itchy patches of eczema on adults as well as babes. Shea Terra sends us carrot seed oil that I use in my homemade face cream along with Mountain Rose's fresh-pressed borage oil. Meg and Isabel watch companies who make lotions and potions like gentle hawks to make sure ingredients are safe.

We order baskets and scarves and lovely things that make life brighter from Fair Trade Companies like Sevya, Serrv, Shupaca and Andes Trading. We carry Big Dipper beeswax candles and divine incense from Nippon Kodo and Juniper Ridge. Cheryl orders Sōa Natural Skin Recovery Soap which lathers, lasts forever, and which is gentle on all kinds of skin but whose sulfur really helps troubled skin. She curates cards from local artists and photographers such as Betsy Mandrioli, Carol Calabro, Jim Leahy—and herself!

We have a strong dietary supplement and herb department, and I personally don't know where I'd be without our supplement companies. They follow Good Manufacturing Practices. They are companies like Natural Factors, Country Life, Life Extension, Carlson Labs, Barleans, Jarrow, New Chapter, Planetary Herbals, Herb Pharm, Gaia, Nordic Naturals, Garden of Life, Probulin, Emerald Labs, Doctors Best, our own private label brands from Vitamer Labs, Vitality Works and Reliance, and many more.

Look in my purse and you'll find the homeopathic liquid called *Accident/Injury* by Newton Homeopathics. I always have Boiron's Oscillo at home in case I feel I'm coming down with something, and apis for bee stings. I rely on Threshold's Systemic Vitamin C and I love Coenzyme B-complexes.

CBD companies are new for us, but we admire them. CV Sciences was the first CBD company on our shelves, and we've added Straight Hemp, Sunsoil and others, all of whom are straight shooters and make honest products.

Adam and Rebecca are believers in Grief Relief by David Winston and his company, Herbalist and Alchemist. Grace says we should never be out of Livercare by Himalaya.

Leaving supplements, chocolate is a category that sets an example and led the way for social activism in the natural products industry. Alter Eco, one of our many outstanding chocolate companies, said that "after seeing the challenges in humanitarian aid efforts, we (founders, Mathieu Senard and Edouard Rollet) have become pioneers in social entrepreneurialism, using our business to fight for economic and social justice. We've baked this dedication into Alter Eco's core values and it's the main reason we source ingredients from farmer-owned co-ops that uphold sustainable agricultural practices. With reforestation and agroforestry, not only are we able to create additional revenue for the farming communities, but crop yields increase."

I enjoy chocolate, and it's a wonderful thing that we can eat good chocolate while helping the world be happier and healthier.

Unfortunately, some companies close and we never know why. Vermont Peanut Butter Company is one such. To this day, we don't know what happened. We and our customers loved their peanut butters. The crunchy was my favorite. They seemed to have difficulty meeting demand, until they suddenly stopped shipping, and then stopped answering their phone or email.

Some companies fade away. We remember Walnut Acres (my mom used to mail order from Walnut Acres before health food stores were everywhere) and Erewhon. Jim Leahy remembers the shock that went through the industry some 40 years ago when Erewhon first introduced brown rice cakes. "Packaged, processed food!" many cried. Today there is no Erewhon and no more Erewhon brown rice cereal, which Jim says first hit the shelves in our stores in 1976.

More recently, Ken and Gina's, a tiny local ice cream company that used organic ingredients and added no gums or stabilizers, went under because people wouldn't pay more for the real deal. I loved their ice cream but couldn't eat my weight in vanilla to keep them going.

So, has our industry changed? Have our companies changed? The short answer is yes. Many of our companies are more corporate. The large chains call the shots and dictate which ingredients are acceptable (i.e. sugar). But every time we go to a show, we're on the lookout for new little brands.

We've had companies gobbled up through mergers and acquisitions as our industry's success attracts outside investors and big money. Arrowhead Mills, DeBoles Pasta and more than 30 other companies became part of Hain Celestial. General Mills acquired Annie's, Inc. for $820 million in September of 2014. The Clorox Company bought Burt's Bees, Coca-Cola Company bought Honest Teas, and Kellogg's owns Kashi. Sunfood and the supplement company, New Chapter, were taken over by Procter & Gamble.

Go to the Proctor and Gamble website and you'll see no mention of Sunfood or New Chapter as P&G companies. You do see Tide and Bounce. My guess is that reason P&G is quiet about their takeover is because they know that their name is mud in our industry.

Mergers and acquisitions are not always a bad thing, if they can help keep these wonderful products on the shelves. But it certainly changes their stories. Adam says, "They're no longer these cute little, passionate companies who are all about health and doing good. Cornucopia Institute, a non-profit research group, chastised more than one brand for cutting corners after they were acquired by corporations. They reported on GMO grains and pesticide residues in Kashi cereal. They lambasted Tom's of Maine toothpaste for crossing the line and sneaking carrageenan into its toothpaste."

I like to think about the positives. I like to think that our companies, once acquired, can effect change in the larger corporation. For instance, when Hormel acquired Applegate, a team at Applegate was charged with initiating sustainable practices for Hormel. It is my hope that new parent companies will become intrigued, understand that their bottom line can be improved by doing good and making products that keep us healthier. That's my Pollyanna-ish take on the matter until proven otherwise. When this doesn't happen, I hope our shops and our shoppers will jump up and down, protest, make phone calls and write letters, and take our business elsewhere.

In the meantime, I'm going to speak to two new little companies who've just introduced themselves and who are hoping like the dickens we'll make room for them on our shelves. We will, and we will need your help keeping them there!

And because we're talked about so many different kinds of food in this chapter, let me end with a quote from Mark Twain. "Part of the secret of success in life is to eat what you like and let the food fight it out inside."

Chapter 9

Have We Ordered Our Turkeys Yet?

In the store, if it's late Summer or the beginning of September, we've already ordered our Thanksgiving Turkeys from Alberts's Organics, and we've reserved our turkey truck, too. We have turkeys to sell. If we don't sell the majority of them at Thanksgiving, we're dead ducks. We don't have the spare freezer space to hold so many birds. I remember the year turkeys just weren't selling, and I was sweating bullets.

Thank goodness for Constant Contact and the customers who responded to my SOS. Frank Yans wrote, "Deb, if you end up with a truckload of 600 unsold turkeys call us, we can always eat two or three more turkeys." Frank and others saved our bacon, as I'm fond of saying. (You can tell Thanksgiving is a meaty time for us, turkeys, ducks and bacon).

Turkeys in our store—and in everyone else's store, too—are a big deal around Thanksgiving. We have a "How to Cook Your Turkey" handout. We have spreadsheets to keep track of the folks who want a Mary's Organic turkey or a Stonewood Natural bird. Heaven help us if someone shows up for their turkey and we don't have their table's centerpiece waiting for them.

Mind you, we order extra turkeys to freeze for our customers who will want a turkey for Christmas or New Years, and so our kitchen can make turkey dinners when it's blustery in January.

Our staff think I over-order. Perhaps I do, but that's because I remember the year we didn't have enough to fill our orders.

That year is still a cautionary tale for our staff to remind everyone to take orders carefully, and make sure we don't sell more than we're getting. That year, when we realized we had six turkeys left, but 14 people who were still coming in for their bird, Mom and my brother David, who had flown in from California for the holiday, raced to Whole Foods to buy enough turkeys to fill our orders. We were unbelievably lucky that Whole Foods still had turkeys for sale, and so, even though we knew this wasn't a sustainable business model, we snapped them up and made our customers happy. Needless to say, we 'fessed up and didn't charge them for those organic birds that weren't ours. Those customers that year left our store feeling that we had their backs.

In the early years, because he always came to Concord for Thanksgiving, we pressed my Brudder David into service. He and Jim, our store manager, did the heavy lifting and gave turkeys to their rightful owners as they arrived, one after the other.

David has a peculiar sense of humor. One year he decided it would be funny to name each bird and hand him or her over with a family history. This horrified our customers. Imagine the face of a vegetarian customer who was buying a turkey to make her family happy when

David said, "Hi. This is Gertrude. She likes ruffled aprons." Or, "Sadie, the turkey, is partial to parsnips." "Harold prefers to be buttered."

To this day, there are some people, who beg us not to name their turkeys. They prefer the anonymity. They don't want to know that "Ralph is gluten-free and doesn't do gravy." Or that their bird is named Henry or Harry or Hortense!

That year, however, was still a piece of cake compared to the first year when we ordered organic birds from a farmer (my lips are sealed, and I will take his name to my grave to protect the not-so-innocent) who lived in western Massachusetts. I ordered turkeys in distinct size ranges, and we had an agreement in writing. When the turkeys arrived that first year, it was clear that the farmer had never worked with a retailer. The birds arrived with pin feathers (think turkeys on the prairie that need plucking) and not a one under 25 pounds. The largest bird topped the scale at 35 or 36 pounds. My memory is a little fuzzy. But the average size ordered by our early, brave band of customers was around 18 pounds.

In horror, when I pointed out the discrepancy between what we ordered and what was delivered, the farmer replied that the birds just wouldn't stop eating. I was such a retail greenhorn that it didn't occur to me to refuse the delivery and throw myself on the mercy of those who were counting on us for their turkeys. We could have sent them to Bob's Turkey Farm and paid for their birds.

Think about a 35-pound turkey. Many people do not have ovens that will hold a bird that large. No one would want to pay for those extra pounds of turkey either. It was, of course, a fiasco. Ninety-nine percent of the folks who had trusted us to have their birds ready for pick up the Tuesday before Thanksgiving were hysterical. They scrambled to come up with a backup plan, and we did send them to Bob's or Shaw's or wherever else might have extras. Some, even though we offered to pay for their turkey, which they would buy elsewhere, never returned to our shop. And we were still stuck with about 20 humongous turkeys.

We donated birds to soup kitchens with large ovens. I took a 35-pounder home, and on Thanksgiving, tucked it snugly into my own oven. It didn't occur to me that the turkey shouldn't touch the oven walls, that it needed room to breathe and for air circulations. My turkey set the oven on fire and the fire department made an impromptu visit to wish me "Happy Thanksgiving!" I will never forget the look on the face of the firemen when they saw the size of my bird. "Holy crap," said one. "That's not a turkey, it's a cow."

I do not remember what we ate that day, but it wasn't turkey. Speaking of firemen, this joke, we understand has much basis in truth:

"A fireman received a call from a woman who asked him how to baste a turkey. After a stunned moment, he, being a fairly good cook, described the procedure. Then he asked, 'But why would you call the fire house to find out how to baste a turkey?'

"There was only a slight hesitation before she replied, 'Well, you knew, didn't you?' and hung up."

Nowadays, our turkeys are killed early to make sure they are ready for all of us when we want them, which is a couple of days before the holiday. That means that around the country, turkeys are "harvested" and then put into a deep chill to keep them fresh and their meat safe to eat before we take them home. When you stop to think about it, there's no other way. Farmers simply could not kill all our turkeys three days before Thanksgiving.

Mary's chooses to chill their turkeys to the legal max. These are, according to the rules and regs, like all other birds processed at that time, fresh turkeys. Mary's takes no chances with our health. And each year, there are a few customers who ask us if their turkeys are really fresh. They don't trust the cold crust and won't believe their turkey isn't frozen.

Mary's writes the following: "Federal law says that fresh turkeys may arrive with a hard, cold layer on the outside of the birds. This is because our turkeys are put through a deep chill blaster as soon as possible after they are packaged. They stay in this deep chill blaster until the internal temperature reaches 26 degrees. Turkey meat does not begin to freeze until the temperature gets below this temperature. This is due to the naturally occurring sodium in meat products. Though cold, a turkey may be labeled as fresh as long as the temperature does not go below 26 degrees.

"If a turkey arrives in your facility in the 26-28-degree range, and has this rather hard surface, it is an indication that both the packer and the trucker have done their jobs well. Studies have proven that quality and flavor are not compromised with this deep chill procedure, and you are ensured that you are providing the safest turkey possible to your customers. You can comfortably and legally inform your customers that this turkey has never been frozen."

Despite this information, which we share, a few people return their "frozen" Mary's turkey with a look. "How dare you try and pass a frozen bird off as fresh!"

Killing turkeys or chickens or any live thing is something that I never know how to talk about. I don't know how to make customers (and staff) who don't believe in killing any living thing feel better. And even though I eat meat, there's a part of me that feels like a bad human being when I do.

Let me apologize to all our vegetarian and vegan customers and vegetarians and vegans everywhere. (A vegetarian doesn't eat anything with a face. A vegan won't either, nor will he or she eat anything animal-related. For instance, she won't eat honey because that means taking honey away from the bees themselves.)

Turkeys are born, they eat, they grow, and we kill them to eat them. I don't know how to justify that.

Speaking of vegetarian, Laughing Water, who owns Real Food Market & Deli in Helena, MT, is a vegetarian. His store is an Independent Natural Food Retailer Association (INFRA) member, like ours. He sent me this turkey story:

> When I think back to our first year of selling fresh turkeys in 2003, I want to cry. It turned out that the turkeys were not refrig-

erated properly by the growers. If you can imagine having your local radio station telling people to bring their turkeys back to your store on Thanksgiving Eve. We gave our customers double their money back for this ultimate grocery store failure, perhaps one of the best returns on investment we've ever seen.

In the end it seems to have been good for our reputation. The local newspaper commended us in an editorial, and now, after that rude introduction to selling fresh turkeys, we seem to be a valued and trusted source. In the end, too, our growers' insurance company picked up the tab, as appropriate, including the double refund. So, I guess that's my Thanksgiving Story. Best to all.

We've certainly had our own challenges with Turkey Day. Back in the day, turkeys would get dropped off in our parking lot, where they would get organized and then covered with a tarp. We were weather-dependent to keep them cold, for there was no way we could fit them all into our walk-in refrigerators in our store's basement. We became religious and prayed to God for cold weather…but not too cold.

These days, we've sort of settled into a rhythm with turkeys over the years. We order them from farms we trust, and we have a distributor who brings them to us. Jim Leahy and Ray Mong ("Farmer Ray," as we call him) used to drive about two hours away to pick up a refrigerated truck to park in our parking lot. When the turkeys were delivered, we hoisted them up in there. The last few years, Albert's Organics, our turkey distributor, has been kind enough to leave us their truck with our turkeys already inside.

We started off with a typed list of people who ordered turkeys. We had no spreadsheet. My brother David—he who reveled in naming turkeys—insisted we use a simple one he created after seeing the madness of our trying to find people's names and not being able to sort by phone number, by name, etc.

Now, when the turkey truck gets parked in the back-parking lot behind the store, our list is sortable backwards and forwards and roundabout. We still sometimes have trouble finding people because our list is only as good as the information taken at the register. If we write down Smith as Mitch, or have a typo in the phone number, we're off to a rocky start.

Speaking of a turkey's weight (which we weren't but now are), they say to allow about a pound and a half of turkey per person. Less if you have small eaters and don't want leftovers. More if you have men who eat a lot and don't finish what they have before reaching for more, and if you want to send family and friends home with turkey doggy bags.

For people whose guests will fight over drumsticks, we suggest people order two mediums or one medium and one small, instead of a huge bird. That way you get double drumsticks and everything else.

When we place our turkey order, we're given ranges of sizes. So a small Mary's might range between 12 and 15 pounds. We don't know exactly what sizes within that range will arrive. It's just the way it is.

We explain this to people when they place their orders. They nod their heads. The truck arrives, and we learn that all the Mary's smalls are 12 pounders this year (a 12-pound turkey is otherwise known as a large chicken). People want what they want. "I ordered a 15-pound turkey. What do you mean you only have a 12 pounder for me? Oh no, that won't do." And we're off to the races to figure out if we can swap out for a Mary's medium, all of which have come in on the larger size of their range.

We feel everyone's pain, we really do. But for the person who's ordered a 20-pound bird and is distraught that the one handed to them is 20.2 pounds, we wish we could hand them a stiff drink. But a pat on the shoulder with a "There, there" is as good as we can do. We want everyone to have a lovely Thanksgiving, but there are some things we can't change.

Here's our old, old, old Thanksgiving handout, in case you are cooking a bird this year and want reassurance.

Wondering how to cook your bird?

Years ago, I read Adele Davis' advice on how to cook a turkey. I've been cooking it that way for years! The breast meat doesn't dry out, and you don't need to worry about basting. Your turkey will be moist and flavorful. I promise. More about that method in a bit.

Step one: Make sure you've got the best quality turkey available, and you've already done that. Congratulations!

You're picking up your turkey Tuesday before Thanksgiving. When you get home, remove turkey from plastic, and wash it out with water. Pull out any remaining feather stubs in the turkey skin. Remove neck and giblets (heart, gizzard, liver). I broil the liver and eat it right away. You can chop the giblets and gizzard for soup or put those right in your freezer if you don't want to be bothered at Thanksgiving. Pat the turkey dry (if you want a crispy skin, this is imperative!)

In a little bowl, mix a tablespoon or two of parsley, sage, rosemary and thyme (I use dried herbs because it's easier for me) together with about eight crushed garlic cloves and ½ C olive oil. Rub turkey inside and out. Cut another few garlic bulbs into slivers and with a sharp knife make some inserts into the meaty portions of the turkey. Insert slivers everywhere. Put seasoned bird into pan and cover, or alternatively, put seasoned bird into a clean plastic garbage bag.

Store turkey in the fridge, or if the weather is cold enough, in the garage or on a porch. If the weather is too cold, store it in the fridge so your turkey doesn't freeze! Wash your work area with hot soapy water and take the same care you do after working with and handling any poultry. Wash your hands too!

Thanksgiving Day. Allow turkey to mellow at room temperature for about two hours. Preheat oven to 400 F. You'll want to cook your turkey **breast-side down** on the bottom of a rack over a sturdy roasting pan big enough to catch all the drippings. Cooking the turkey breast down means the skin over the breast won't be so brown, but as your turkey roasts, juices will fall down and baste the breast, so *you* don't have to. (Of course, you can turn turkey up towards the end so the breast will brown if that's your heart's desire.)

Adele Davis' method of cooking a turkey: Adele Davis said to cook your turkey at 400 F for the first hour, and then turn the oven to warm (225 F). Walk away and leave your turkey in the oven the whole day. Six hours, eight hours, nine hours. Same delicious result. And I've found that to be true.

Traditional method to cook turkey: Cooking time is about 15 minutes for every pound. For a 15-pound turkey, put your bird into that 400 degree for the first half hour. Then reduce the heat to 350 F for the next two hours. Then reduce the heat further to 225 F for the next hour to hour and a half. Baste every couple of hours with juice from pan.

To brine a turkey, Amanda says to dissolve one cup salt and one cup natural sugar in warm water in a pot on stove. Add two quartered oranges, two lemons, six sprigs fresh thyme, four sprigs fresh rosemary and two gallons of water. Let this mixture sit overnight and then brine your turkey in this solution for six to 36 hours. On Thanksgiving, remove the turkey from brine and roast either of the above ways.

No matter how you cook your turkey, when you remove your bird from the oven, let it rest for 15-20 minutes. Turn the turkey breast side up to carve.

Stuffing: Cook your turkey stuffing separately, if you make one (my family never did because my mom liked to roast potatoes, yams, parsnips and carrots instead, and make a separate lentil/wild rice or other whole grain pilaf on the stovetop). In any case, my advice is don't put your stuffing in the turkey cavity because it's easier without it inside. You can cook the turkey more evenly and is less labor-intensive to boot!

While many people close up the turkey cavity with either string (not nylon string!) or metal skewers and tie the legs together, which does result, I have to admit, in a better-looking bird for presentation, I can't be bothered. I pop the whole thing into the roasting rack and let Mr. Turkey sit there comfortably.

Need help figuring out how big a turkey to get? Typically, plan on a pound and a half of turkey per person. I like to go with a larger turkey because it makes a fantastic presentation, and because I like leftovers. After the meal, when the turkey is still warm, it's a snap to pull the meat off the bones and put it into baggies and then pop into the freezer for wonderful soups or sandwiches the rest of the winter.

Thermometer: I don't use a meat thermometer. If *you* do, insert deep into the thickest part of the turkey breast or thigh. White meat in the breast should be 161° F. My method is to lightly spear the breast with a knife. The juices should run clear, not pink. Farmer Ray says the most common mistake is overcooking, because a turkey keeps cooking for an hour after it's out of the oven.

An extra treat here: an appetizer. Serve it with the bird, or serve it as part of a wonderful vegetarian holiday meal. Even mushroom-haters seem to love this one. This is a 30-minute hors d'oeuvre, a wonderful thing in a season that is rushed. Not much muss, definitely gourmet. Will they say "Wow?" You bet!

Leftovers can be spooned over beans, a grain, fish or eggs. Spoon over polenta or pasta, roll in steamed chard leaves. Or serve as a side dish as is. Top a mixed green salad. Your way, babe.

If you want to know something of the history of mushrooms, they go way back. Mushrooms were prized by the Pharaohs as a delicacy, by the Greeks to provide strength for warriors in battle, and by the Romans who served them only on holidays because they were regarded as a gift from God. The Chinese treasure mushrooms as a giver of health and protector of immunity.

Mixed Mushroom Cups

Serves about 8-10 happy people

¼ C extra virgin olive oil	1 tsp dried tarragon
2 Tbsp ghee, butter or coconut oil	2 tsp good salt
½ lb shiitakes, sliced ¼-inch thick	1 tsp ground pepper
½ lb maitakes, coarse crumbled	Rustic sourdough bread
½ lb other 'rooms, sliced ½-inch thick	Enough extra virgin olive oil to
6 cloves garlic, pressed	brush, drizzle
2 Tbsp lemon juice	snipped chives or minced scallions
1 tsp dried thyme	as garnish

In a large skillet, gently warm the extra virgin olive oil and ghee (or butter or coconut oil). Add mushrooms and cook over moderately high heat, stirring, until browned, about 4 minutes. Add garlic, lemon juice and herbs and spices and cook until fragrant, about 2 minutes.

Slice the bread, if using, into half-inch rounds. Light a grill or preheat a grill pan. Brush the bread with extra virgin olive oil and grill until toasted and charred in spots, about 1 minute per side.

Spoon the mushrooms on top of the toast. Garnish with snipped chives or minced scallions. Cut each toast slice (crostini) in half, drizzle with more olive oil and serve.

May your Thanksgiving be delicious and spent with those you love. May your home be fragrant, and may there be light, health and happiness. Love from all of us here at the store.

• •

Chapter 10

Distractions And Taking Up Causes

I have always wanted to change the world. Issues like food waste and hanging laundry outside get me charged up. I feel compelled to share my cause of the moment, and the store newsletter is the perfect vehicle. I get such a kick, giddy almost, imagining our readers, inspired, taking action and forwarding our newsletter to friends around the country and across the big pond. Maybe I'm naïve. But I have at times been dazzled by the power of the press. I've seen what can happen if enough people with good will and conviction work together. Great things can happen.

Our customers and vendors sometimes laugh at me, but some listen up. Some started hanging laundry out, at least until the snow flew, after my call to action in 2010. Others of our shoppers, however, throw up their hands. "There she goes again," I hear them mutter. "Dust the shelves instead," said one aggravated regular.

Laundry And A Call To Action: At Concord's annual town meeting Peggy Brace agitated for hanging laundry out to dry. Why? Well, Peggy reminded us all that hanging laundry outside to dry uses simple technology, and saves energy, which saves us money. Clothes last longer, too, when you skip the electric dryer (no lint is tumbled out). Sunlight disinfects clothes and bleaches out stains, and laundry hung outside smells fresh without artificial, stinky dryer sheets. Peggy reminded us that using an indoor rack to dry clothes in the winter helps humidify the house.

So this inspired me. My mother always hung her laundry outside, 365 days a year. What started out as a personal self-improvement project is morphing into a "Call to Action."

I'd like to issue a challenge to all of us to think differently about how we do everyday things. Personally, if I change my behavior one day a week, it might be easier to change it twice weekly, and so on until I'm living more simply. And saving money. Paying less for electricity would mean more money to pay off loans or spend on fun stuff, wouldn't it?

What would you add to the list I've started below, and would you like to work on a Call to Action with me?

Monday: hang laundry outside; Tuesday: go to bed when it gets dark; Wednesday: walk or bike somewhere leaving the car in the driveway; Thursday: make a meal that uses mostly local and organic ingredients; Friday: bring water wherever I go in a stainless or glass bottle or jar; Saturday: eat lower on the food chain, no meat; Sunday: substitute vinegar for general kitchen cleansers (vinegar kills germs and isn't harmful to humans or pets). Try a bit of baking soda when an abrasive is needed.

We all know the stuff that's easier to do like using energy-saving light bulbs, or not holding open a refrigerator while you decide what you want from the inside. But where can we go from there?

A suggestion: go to Vanderhoof's Hardware, 28 Main Street, Concord. Buy a clothes-drying rack. They have every kind, from the simple wooden racks to the kind my mother used to have in her backyard set in poured concrete like a promise to the world!

Dietary Supplements: DSHEA. Instead of dusting shelves, we found ourselves on the front page of the business section of the *Boston Globe* during the national campaign to pass the Federal Dietary Supplement Health and Education Act of 1994 (DSHEA).

Our shop generated so many letters to Congress in support of DSHEA, that it became news. And just after we were in the paper, as I was riding an up escalator at the Javits Center in New York City, I heard a group of suits riding the down escalator hollering over to ask if it was I who had been in the paper. Our minute of fame. No fortune, though.

DSHEA, as written on the federal government's website, was "enacted by Congress following public debate concerning the importance of dietary supplements in promoting health, the need for consumers to have access to current and accurate information about supplements, and controversy over the Food and Drug Administration's (FDA) regulatory approach to this product category."

Our shop had speakers, wrote columns and provided a forum for discussion. We provided paper, envelopes and stamps so people could write letters of support on the spot. Strike while the iron is hot, is my motto.

Signing DSHEA into law on October 25, 1994, President Clinton said: "After several years of intense efforts, manufacturers, experts in nutrition and legislators, acting in a conscientious alliance with consumers at the grassroots level, have moved successfully to bring common sense to the treatment of dietary supplements under regulation and law."

I heard that the government got more letters on DSHEA than on any other issue up to that time. It was a lesson in democracy that we, the people, do have power some of the time!

Stevia, Sweet Plant. From DSHEA to stevia in one giant leap: stevia gave us and many people around the country the chance to learn how our government agencies work—in this case, the FDA. Stevia afforded our shop a glimpse into the way lobbying and politics affects the food chain.

The FDA, in the early days of our store, said "No!" to stevia. Stevia, as you know, tastes many times sweeter than sugar without affecting blood sugar. It has zero calories. It's been used safely since the beginning of time. It's not addictive and you can't smoke it.

I grow stevia in my garden so the neighborhood kids can taste. Persuading them to pop something green and leafy into their mouths isn't easy, but watching a child's eyes widen as the explosion of sweet hits their taste buds is great fun.

It was dismaying, then, in 2007, when the FDA, under pressure from the powerful sugar and artificial sweetener lobby, issued a warning letter to Celestial Seasonings for using stevia in some of its teas. The letter said stevia was "unsafe."

In their letter to Celestial Seasonings, the FDA stated that "enforcement action may include seizure of violative products." The FDA did enforce a ban at the border on stevia. They detained imported food products that contained it.

The FDA publicly claimed that no evidence had been provided to them about stevia's safety, but in fact federal records proved the FDA had received more than a thousand scientific studies. All but one said stevia was safe.

To put things in perspective, in contrast, half the studies provided to the FDA regarding the artificial sweetener aspartame warn of serious health concerns, yet aspartame is alive and well in our country.

Today, because "the people" spoke up and exercised our civic right to speak out, stevia is legal. Today some major corporations have their own versions of stevia-based sugar substitutes. One, developed jointly and introduced to the public in 2008 by The Coca-Cola Company and Cargill, is also alive and well. However, Truvia, as it's called, uses a sweet compound isolated from the stevia plant ("Rebiana" on the label), erythritol, which is a sugar alcohol, and natural flavors. The manufacturer does not specify what those natural flavors actually are. The Coca-Cola Company filed 24 domestic patent applications for Rebiana in everything from vitamins to cereal.

Coke took the stevia plant, which could not be patented, created a modified substitute they could patent, got exclusive rights to it, and started charging an arm and a leg!

The whole stevia plant does have health properties. In my opinion, the monkeyed-around-with Truvia does not.

Beating the drum for our right to use stevia was like David taking on Goliath, but it was worth it. That battle was part of why our shoppers trust us.

Jane and Algernon, shoppers in our store, may not care about every cause we take up on all our behalves, but to this day they love this recipe for stevia lemonade. Thanks to Adam, we've been enjoying this recipe for years. And, yes, it can also be found in our third cookbook: *Blue Ribbon Edition, From Our Kitchen To Yours.*

An 8-ounce cup of Pink Stevia Lemonade yields roughly three calories. You can live it up, baby!

Adam wrote, "Hibiscus is a beautiful flower and makes a pretty tea and lemonade, but does it have health benefits? There are consistent scientific studies that show hibiscus helps with hypertension and liver disorders. One study, published in 2004 in the journal *Phytomedicine* (2004;11:375–82), concluded that 'people suffering from hypertension can lower their blood pressure significantly by drinking hibiscus tea daily. The study included 70 people–one half of whom drank 16-oz of hibiscus tea before breakfast daily. The other half ingested 25 mg of an antihypertensive medication (*captopril*) twice daily. After one month, the hibiscus tea drinkers' diastolic blood pressure was reduced by at least ten points in 79 percent of participants; blood pressure in the medicated group was reduced by at least ten points in some 84 percent of participants–a statistically insignificant difference.' And, hibiscus tea is caffeine-free, rich in vitamin C and known to act as a natural body refrigerant in North Africa. All the more reason to enjoy it in the Summertime."

Hibiscus Stevia Lemonade

Makes 1 gallon

2 Traditional Medicinals brand	1 tsp NuNaturals brand pure
hibiscus tea bags	stevia extract*
¾ C organic lemon juice	1 gallon water

Pour about 8 cups boiling water over hibiscus tea bags. Steep at least 5 minutes. Add ¾ cups lemon juice and 1 tsp pure stevia extract powder (make sure you're getting the pure extract). Add water to make 1 gallon total. Chill. You'll love both taste and color!

Variation #1: Replace hibiscus with your favorite fruit or berry tea bags (elderberry, perhaps?)

Variation #2: Use fizzy mineral water instead of water.

Variation #3: Roughly double stevia and lemon to make popsicles.

Pure stevia extract is much sweeter than stevia products that contain maltodextrin, or other added ingredients. We've carried the one from NuNaturals for years.

• •

Food Waste. When we opened the shop in 1989, it never occurred to me that we'd have to struggle with the issue of waste. But truth be told, waste is a never-ending saga. We struggle to address waste both in the shop and in our own homes.

Which makes me think of celery leaves. I remember being shocked when I saw people in our kitchen, in the early days, throwing away celery leaves because they didn't know you could eat them! Today I throw celery leaves from my garden right into my Vitamix and blend with parsley stems, a pinch of basil and some mint, which makes a refreshing green drink.

Years ago, I had an interesting conversation with Stephan Dorlandt, founder of a company that made coffee leaf tea that we used to sell. We stopped selling it because even with articles in our newsletter and signs at the shelf, folks didn't buy it.

I've lost touch with Stephan. His mission was to educate people about the tons and tons of edible leaves that we throw away. He says using leaves exemplify "cycling;" that is, using something that's already here but not being used.

Coffee leaves, for instance, have more antioxidants and vitamins than coffee beans, Stephan said. They have less acid than coffee and are caffeine-free. Coffee tea was drunk thousands of years before roasting coffee beans was invented.

I keep banging the drum to get us all to recognize that leaves are plant organs, which work hard at photosynthesis and have more phytonutrients that other parts of plants and trees. They're not just ornamental.

For instance, the Department of Agriculture database says that beet leaves have more vitamin A, vitamin C, vitamin E, vitamin B-1, vitamin B-2, niacin, calcium, potassium, omega-3s, and protein than the beet roots we eat.

Stephen used to tell me that perhaps "the single most important thing we can do to help end world hunger (not to mention malnutrition and obesity) is to start eating the millions of tons of edible leaves we throw away each year!"

How many of us eat edible leaves? I bet I'm not the only one who doesn't eat strawberry leaves, carrot tops and cucumber leaves. I know our kitchen cuts off tops of sprouting onions and puts them in the bin for chickens.

Recently, I got wildly excited about using banana peels to make faux bacon. It works! Even though we give all our banana peels to customers who give them to their animals, it kills me to see all those peels not being used as human food. If you think I'm off my rocker, just read the blogs online. In other parts of the world, people do eat the banana, peel and all. There are recipes for vegan pulled pork using banana skins as the main ingredient. Banana peel bacon is incredibly delicious. Ask our staff. They rolled their eyes when I proposed trying the recipe. No one took me up on the idea, but they loved it when I made it and brought it into the store. There wasn't a nibble left for rabbits.

Banana Peel "Bacon"

In this recipe, make sure you're using ripe bananas. You want to see brown spots on the peels!

Makes enough for 4 people (more if you're only nibbling or using to crumble on top of a salad as garnish)

4 banana peels (from 4 bananas)	½ tsp smoked paprika
3 Tbsp soy sauce	½ tsp garlic powder
1 Tbsp maple syrup	2-3 Tbsp extra virgin olive oil

Rinse bananas. Peel them. Using a spoon, scrape off the white inside part of the peel. We're using the peel only. Slice or tear each banana peel into 4 strips lengthwise.

In a dish large enough to hold your banana peels, mix soy sauce, maple syrup, paprika and garlic powder, which is your marinade. Add peel to marinade and toss to coat. Let peels marinade at room temperature for at least 10 minutes, but a few hours are even better.

When ready to cook bacon, heat oil over medium in a large skillet or frying pan. I used my cast iron skillet. Add peels and fry each a couple of minutes per side until they turn golden and the skin bubbles. I used a pair of tongs to pick up a peel and turn it over. Don't overcook and burn as I did!

Remove banana bacon from pan onto serving plate. These get crispier as they cool.

• •

Household Cleaning Products. Over the years, we've watched folks gallop by our shop's curated detergents and dish soaps. Natural cleaning products do not fly off the shelves, and more and more people come into our store smelling of synthetic fragrance from their laundry products. This despite the fact that our beloved customers eat organic and don't spray their yards with pesticides. It's a societal shift created by watching too many ads about sniffing clothes on television.

And I realize that I am completely unmoored by those fake smells. Imagine my horror to learn that one of my brothers used scented Tide. I wrote this after a visit to his home in 2018:

Tide and Good-Bye Simple Life. It's getting harder and harder to live a simple life. I'm not talking about politics. I'm talking about being able to take a walk without having to breathe in the fumes from people's laundry. I'm talking about being subjected to the smell of people's detergent and dryer sheets when you go anywhere in public.

Advertisements show people swooning over a towel after it's been washed. They show folks taking ecstatic breaths when their clothes come out of the dryer.

Oh, my goodness. Did you know that cleaning products are not required by law to list all ingredients on the box? "Fragrance," listed as a single ingredient, can contain up to 200 chemicals.

In an article called *Toxic Laundry* by Hiyaguha Cohen, she relates a study in which laundry got washed "with the scented detergent and then run through the dryer with a popular brand of scented dryer sheets. The scientists monitored the emissions coming from the dryers during each laundry load. After analysis, it turned out that the dryer vents emitted 25 volatile organic compounds (VOCs)…chemical compounds that can cause long-term health effects. The EPA classifies seven of the VOCs as hazardous air pollutants, and two—acetaldehyde and benzene—as carcinogens with no safe exposure level. In other words, even a small whiff of dryer fumes once in a blue moon can cause health problems.

"When both dryer sheets and the scented laundry were used, the emissions contained 17 more VOCs, including acetaldehyde, acetone, benzaldehyde, butanal, dodecane, hexanal, limonene, nonanal, octanal, tetramethylpropylidene cyclopropane, 1-(1,1-dimethylethyl)-4-ethylbenzene, 1-propanal, 2-butanone, and 2,7-dimethyl-2,7-octanediol …

"According to study director Anne Steinemann, 'These products can affect not only personal health, but also public and environmental health. The chemicals can go into the air, down the drain and into water bodies.'

I recently had an experience with one detergent, Tide. Here's the letter I wrote to the CEO of Tide (Proctor & Gamble) on December 13, 2018:

> Dear Mr. Taylor, I use safe cleaning products in my home. Two weeks ago, however, I visited my brother in Asheville, NC and used a bottle of Tide liquid laundry detergent he had in his home.

I'd like to know what ingredients in that product won't wash out, won't dissipate even though I've washed my clothes here at home four times, and each time afterwards hung those clothes outside on my line, where they are right now.

My clothes included a 100 percent merino wool sweater, a pair of Nike fleece-lined exercise pants, underwear that is nylon, some that is organic cotton, and Darn Tough socks.

I can't bring the clothes inside because they still smell of whatever synthetic perfume is in that liquid Tide. The fake smell is simply awful!

I am more concerned about the effect of those chemicals on my skin. I am concerned what happens to lungs when the chemicals are breathed in. I would like to know what I'm dealing with, what might remove the chemical from my clothes. I've tried vinegar, soap, baking soda, all to no avail.

Thank you, Debra Stark

I've washed those clothes 14 more times and have continued hanging them outside between washes. They still smell of fragrance from Tide. Yes, the *Consumer Care* office at Proctor & Gamble answered my letter and wrote that they list their ingredients on their website. As directed, I went there and looked, but there were no ingredients for fragrance! When I wrote them back about this, *Consumer Care* went silent. Call to action! If, like me, you want to live a simpler life, contact manufacturers. Consumer opinion can have a real impact and create a shift. A good brand image is important to every business. Make companies accountable, make them change so you can live more simply.

Genetically Modified Organisms and Corn. Speaking of living simply, oh my goodness, genetically modified organisms (GMOs). This subject makes my head spin, but it informs our purchasing behavior in the shop each and every day.

Suffice it to say that GMOs alter genetic material in an organism in a way that doesn't occur when we select the strongest plant in the field and save its seeds. A tomato may be genetically engineered when its genes are artificially combined with a soybean or a flounder (remember the FLAVR SAVR Tomato?) Cows naturally mate with cows. With genetic engineering, a cow could be crossed with a sheep or a beet.

But simplifying, Monsanto developed GM seeds because their best-selling herbicide called Roundup indiscriminately kills all plants, not just weeds. GM seeds were developed to be Roundup resistant. You could gas an entire field, and the only plants left standing would be Monsanto's.

And what scares the heck out of me today is that those GM seeds blow with the wind and contaminate organic fields. You may have heard of Monsanto suing farmers for "stealing" their GM seeds simply because Mother Nature planted them in unapproved fields. This is true.

If you want to read our article on GMOs, it's on our website.

Instead, here, let me share this funny story:

In the month of October, we usually put in a window about genetically-modified (GM) food (we're not fans). One year I had the brilliant idea to put two full-size shopping carts in the window. We have large windows. I would fill one cart with foods that contain GM ingredients, and the other with similar foods that we sell that have been verified Non-GMO.

I drove 40 minutes away to a supermarket and filled my shopping card with Twinkies, Honey Bunches of Oats, Special K, Jiffy Peanut Butter, cornstarch, and lots of Halloween candy. I drove that distance because I didn't want anyone to see me buying that no-good junk food.

As I was slinking about the store, I heard, "Debra, what are you doing here?!?" A customer of ours. "What the heck? I didn't know you eat crap!" Altogether, four of our customers (what were they doing at Market Basket in the first place, I asked myself) caught me with a cart full of un-eatables. It was not my finest hour, even though I tried to explain. The windows, however, were visually perfect.

Raw Almonds. And just when things seem to be calming down, food-wise, we learn another crop or product is endangered or changed. Enter, almonds. Yes, almonds.

In 2007, the USDA wrote a decision to ban truly raw almonds. Because of this decision, any domestic almond shelled after September first was required to be "pasteurized" either with steam heat or the fumigant, propylene glycol (PPO). Mind you, PPO is a probable human carcinogen. Almonds treated with PPO are banned in Canada and the European Union.

But the USDA allows almond growers and processors to label these treated almonds as "raw" even though they're not. Which makes us confident (hah!) about US truth in labeling.

I was heartened to learn there's integrity in how our farmers and our small organic and natural companies and distributors do business. They committed to selling only heat-treated almonds, not almonds "pasteurized" with PPO. Yay for the good guys!

The funny thing is the USDA/Almond Board of California regulation doesn't require *imported* almonds to be "pasteurized." Therefore, in our store, our truly raw almonds come from Italy and Spain, and that is fine since these countries have wonderful food. These imported raw almonds are called heirloom almonds by the folks that sell them, and they are not as sweet as California almonds. They have a more intense flavor. You get some kernels in almost every batch that are bitter.

I want to weep for our California almond farmers who cannot sell truly raw almonds to us anymore.

How all this passed without public notice or public discussion amazes me. The USDA said it was a food safety issue. They were mum until the very end, gave a scant 30 days for public comment and raced to make a final decision.

When have you ever known the government to move that quickly?

It's said that the company who manufactures propylene oxide had been agitating for use of their product for some years and stood to make a bundle. Two incidents of salmonella were the reason given to make the decision a fait accompli.

Interestingly, the salmonella may not have been the almond's fault. Evidence points to piles of manure on property lines from neighboring farms that factory-farm their animals. Rain is thought to have spread the contamination.

Rainbow Light. Some distractions hurt more than others because they're personal. They go to the heart of our industry, which is being able to trust one another.

In 2017, Adam made the unusual step of posting our concerns about the supplement company Rainbow Light on social media. Rainbow Light was a company we had respected. We sold their products almost from the day the store opened.

"You're looking at a photo of the last of our Rainbow Light products, in the dumpster behind the store. We no longer feel safe selling them."

Adam wrote that, among other things, lab documents from the company itself showed potentially unsafe variances from label claim. Rainbow Light refused to address our worries about the purity of a particular raw material used by a number of manufacturers, including Rainbow Light.

"We take these things seriously at Debra's. So, we requested certificates of analysis (COAs) from all the companies we dealt with that used this ingredient. While the other COAs we received appeared credible, Rainbow's immediately raised red flags: simply put, the lab results were too perfect to be true—everything accurate to the hundredth of a milligram. That simply doesn't happen in the real world."

Adam continued, "Fast forward to June of 2017, when Rainbow again brought a product to market using a similar raw material. Rainbow initially offered to provide a COA, but then later balked, asserting that their lab work was now 'confidential.' (Note: no other company we've encountered makes such a claim). Most troubling of all, despite repeated insistence that the company rigorously tests for heavy metals like mercury, arsenic, cadmium and lead—all of which are anticipated with this type of raw material—these test results were entirely omitted from the COA. This for a product marketing explicitly to pregnant women."

You can find Adam's whole article on this on our website, www.DebrasNaturalGourmet.com.

Our most recent update from Adam on Rainbow Light is the following from 2019: "BREAKING NEWS: almost two years ago, we took the last of our Rainbow Light vitamins to the dumpster, after uncovering a pattern of fraudulently misreported lab work surrounding heavy metal levels in some of their prenatal products. This was a last resort for us. We'd been pushing this issue with them doggedly but kept running up against a brick wall where they insisted there was no wrongdoing, and everything was fine. Today, the company agreed to a $1.75 million settlement with the city of Los Angeles for basically the same transgressions.

"This isn't about us. But I do just want to say, we were in the trenches fighting on this one before anyone else noticed. This wasn't the first time, and it won't be the last."

Not the Last Hurrah. We're all are on the same page about single-use plastic bags. There's no doubt about that. I love what a Canadian independent natural product store called East West Market did to get the message (single-use plastic bags = bad) across, to make sure their customers don't leave their own totes at home. East West Market had their bags printed with slogans like "Dr. Toew's Wart Ointment Wholesale," "The Colon Care Co-op," and "Into the Weird Adult Video Emporium." At the bottom of each bag they printed: "Avoid the shame. Bring a reusable bag." Isn't that a hoot?

Lord love a duck, distractions in our shop and in our industry make us who we are. They make us and the neighborhood a little wacky. I submit they're part of the reason we're lovable.

Chapter 11

Stark Sisters Granola, Originally Debra's Gourmet Granola

The short version of this story is that big wigs from our major distributor (then Cornucopia Natural Foods, now UNFI) came into the store one day. Rick Antonelli, whom I have grown to adore over the years, sniffed the air, and said, "What is that smell?" He meant "smell" in a good way. Within a short period of time Cornucopia placed an order for a pallet of what was then called "Debra's Gourmet Granola." The name "Stark Sisters Granola" came later.

In one weekend, instead of buying a car, I rented a decrepit space in a now razed building behind the store, bought a rotary convection oven and a rolling rack that held 21 sheet pan trays. It was wonderful!

I also bought 21 large stainless-steel mixing bowls at K-Mart, and some strong super-duper rubber spatulas. I called Frank Ford, who founded Arrowhead Mills in 1960 in Hereford, the seat of Deaf Smith County in the southern Texas Panhandle west of Amarillo, Texas. Frank was a stately gentleman who held doors for women, and he immediately said yes to shipping me pallets of organic wheat, rye and barley flakes, and a couple of tons of rolled oats for good measure. I phoned Stuart McFarland at Butternut Mountain Farms and ordered drums that each held 1,000 pounds of the darkest, richest maple syrup, and voilà, I was in the wholesale granola business.

In those early, heady days, I'd work in the store during the day and then trot out our back door over to the factory on Beharrel Street. I'd measure and stir ingredients in each of those 21 bowls at night. When the syrup, oil and pure vanilla extract hit the grain in the bowls, the mixture became unbelievably heavy and my arms, in those days, were Michelle Obama-shapely. Tipping granola out of bowls onto sheet pans and lifting the pans into the grooves of the rolling rack allowed me to eat calories up the wazoo.

Eventually I had to hire helpers so I could sleep, and production moved to daytime. As the granola roasted, West Concord smelled of warm syrup maple, almonds and vanilla. It reminded me of childhood visits to Hershey, PA, where you breathed in chocolate and your skin felt soft with it.

People walking the sidewalks in West Concord, strolled with heads up, sniffing. Happy. If one could have bottled that smell, we'd have made a fortune, and I'd be rich today.

Instead of a fortune, I made mistakes. So many mistakes. For instance, I didn't realize that granola was a commodity product, and that people who buy granola in health food stores like to scoop from bins. They don't want pretty packages.

Bulk is actually pretty simple. The granola gets roasted, then poured, 25 pounds at a time, into heavy-duty plastic bags which have been inserted into a corrugated cardboard box. The bag gets securely twist-tied.

But packaging. I never should have packaged granola at all. But I did and the first rendition of packages were decorated with my brother David's beautiful label. The nutritional information was correct. Used a lab in DC. Check. Label formatting done according to FDA standards. Homework done. Check. But the cellophane bags onto which we affixed the label didn't sit up on a shelf. As a matter of fact, the bags slid right off shelves like lemmings to the sea.

When our bags hit the floor, they shattered as if they were glass. Our first two deliveries to our distributor were a total loss. Thousands of dollars. The exact amount is still too painful for me to consider, and the bags that didn't hit the floor degraded quickly. Did I mention they also ripped?

Round two of packaging, because I am a glutton for punishment, was much better. David designed a wax-lined, earthy-crunchy brown coffee bag with a clear window so people could see the nuts and berries, and there was lots of room on the bags to tell our story. These sat smartly on shelves. They sat even as buyers at the Fancy Food Show in New York City picked them up and said "Great packaging," but didn't care to taste or buy for their stores.

After spending thousands on bags and labels, bulk is what we ended up doing because bulk granola made people feel as if they'd gone back to the land. They'd sing "Oh Susanna" as they scooped. I still have labels and prototypes of our bags at home as souvenirs if you care to see them.

For a time, Stark Sisters Granola was national, and I flew around the country doing tastings. We had distribution up and down the east coast, on the west coast and some places in between. During that period, but after bulk had taken off, Glenn Rifkin, who is a wonderful writer and a friend, reviewed our granola for the *New York Times*. When his column appeared, the phones rang off the hook, and I literally slept in the granola factory for about a week and did nothing but talk to people from around the country who'd read Glenn's piece. I think we filled more than a thousand mail orders in that time, and many of those customers stayed with us for years. If you ever think newspapers are a thing of the past, get reviewed in the *NYT*!

One of those customers, who stayed with us until Stark Sisters closed in 2019, would call and whisper his mail order to me. He didn't want his parrot to hear they were almost out because the parrot would, he said, go ballistic.

Roberta Hershon, another friend who was then a marketing guru for food companies, got us mentioned in *Bon Appetit, The Boston Globe* and again in the *New York Times* (Marian Burros' list for best food gifts for the holidays). This created more buzz and more loyal mail order customers. We got a chance to use up many of the coffee bag packages that David designed.

I don't remember the exact sequence, but at some point, I decided the store was my love child, and I didn't enjoy being a manufacturer. I couldn't do the store and granola both without killing myself. Before or after that, I received a warning letter from Little Debbie's (the company that makes Hostess cupcakes) to cease and desist using the name

I was still using then, Debra's Gourmet Granola. Little Debbie's was busy putting another company called Debbie's Famous Granola out of business by slaughtering them in court, and we were next. Little Debbie was considering getting into the granola business, and they didn't want consumers to buy the wrong granola.

The story of that battle appeared in an article in the *Orlando Sentinel* in 1994, called "Dueling Debbies–The Granola War Is On." Right or wrong, there was no way I could endure the financial pain that put Debbie's Famous out of business. A former sister-in-law, Mary Stark, asked to come into the business with me and suggested the name Stark Sisters Granola. It seemed fortuitous and perfect timing. Neither of us had a sister, and we both had always wanted one, and by changing the company's name, we could outsmart Little Debbie's. Thus also began our adventure to find a co-packer (that's what you call an outfit that makes your product for you). I could not continue to fly back and forth from the store to our manufacturing facility on Beharrell Street. I did not have a death wish.

In those days when we mixed by hand in West Concord, our granola was beautiful. None of the ingredients were damaged by mechanical mixing. The almond slices were huge. We used whole halves of pecans and walnuts for our Nutty Maple Molasses.

Our first co-packer in Pennsylvania would call and threaten us for various and sundry reasons. Order too small. "What the hell?!?" she'd scream. Order too large. "Who do you think I am? Wonder Woman?" she'd shout. Of course, she never paid for my rotary convection oven she trucked down to PA. We kept some of her calls on our answering machine for a few years because they were so entertaining. Then we moved production to New England Natural Bakers (NENB) in Western Mass. Those folks had integrity and a work ethic to be admired.

Mary and I closed down Stark Sisters after some years because a long-distance partnership was tough. It seemed final until Vivian Rush, my beloved retired accountant, who knows more about me than anyone alive, over Chinese food one evening said, "You have an honest co-packer. Why not just start Stark Sisters up again? See where it goes. Maybe it'll pay some bills."

So, I did open the company again solo, just as I had begun. And Stark Sisters did pay some bills and was able to bail the store out of financial difficulties twice. But this second time around was harder. We no longer had national distribution, and I wasn't willing to go flying around, making sales' calls or doing demos. Stark Sisters was an orphan.

And there were still the usual aggravations one has to handle when dealing with any food business, such as the occasional scam artist looking to get rich quick at someone else's expense. Take the consumer who went to the bulk bins at Whole Foods in Bedford, MA and mixed a few granolas together and just happened to put our product number (PLU) on the tag. I don't know how she introduced glass into the bag, but she did. She then went to customer service, threatening to sue. Luckily, Whole Foods called me. Luckily, I live within twenty minutes' drive of Bedford and was able to high-tail it over there. I knew NENB didn't use glass in their manufacturing facility, and I knew that something wasn't kosher. It wasn't. All I had to do was look at the bag and point out that there were ingredients we didn't use. Raisins, for one. We were off the hook, and I hope Whole Foods called the police.

I kept the company open because people continued to write, to call, to say our granola was their favorite. And more people with critters kept calling, too. I don't know why animals liked our granola, it's purely a mystery to me. Maybe animals like pure vanilla? They say a beaver's butt emits a goo called castoreum, that instead of smelling icky, has a musky, vanilla scent, which is why food scientists like to incorporate it in recipes. The FDA regards castoreum as "natural flavoring." We never used beaver butt goo, I swear. On a stack of Bibles. Which is one reason I fought against the regulation that wanted us to use the wording "natural flavoring" on our labels.

Gary from Florida wrote in 2016:

> Hi Debra, my dogs and I love your granola. I have been eating granola since my hippie days in Ann Arbor in the seventies. I used to make it when I could not get good stuff like yours and I had the time.
>
> My dogs will only eat your granola. I guess I spoiled them. They look forward to their granola every morning and evening. Most of that stuff out there they call granola is pretty bad compared to yours. Keep it coming, Gary.

Whole Foods was our largest customer for years, and they were the reason we had distribution around the country. When Whole Foods' Southern region mandated no granolas that would sell for more than $1.99 per pound (yes, this was a long time ago), we lost our bins. When another Whole Foods region's revolving door had bulk managers moving around like hockey pucks, we lost bins. And most recently, when Amazon bought Whole Foods, the decision was made to work with national brands. We lost bins.

I decided to close Stark Sisters, said goodbye in our store's June 2019 newsletter.

Goodbye, Stark Sisters Granola!

It's been 25 years. A quarter century. It's been a good run. But we're closing the doors on my Stark Sisters granola. We were beloved in Concord, and distributed coast to coast!

Back in the day, we were the only granola to sweeten all five flavors with pure maple syrup. Back in the day, we stirred by hand back on Beharrell Street. I'd run back and forth between the store and our granola factory, and it was a grand adventure. At one point we were padlocked by a government agency because our label said, "pure vanilla extract," which, as it turned out, was against the law. One had to say, "natural flavors," or list all the sub-ingredients of vanilla extract.

Our granolas were visually gorgeous because we stirred by hand, slow roasted and left crunchy chunks. The taste was, of course, delicious.

Over the years we outgrew our space on Beharrell and moved to a co-packer. They were able to keep the taste, but we lost the chunks because the granola was mixed by machine. To keep prices affordable, we cut a few *tiny* corners. Almonds, for example, went from thick slices to small bits. No big deal, maybe. But when we received another letter this spring saying we had to cut costs again, in a big way, or raise our prices in a big way, we couldn't justify it anymore.

Yes, those recipes can still be found in our cookbooks (in home-sized batches) and we hope you have them all because we like talking to you through our recipes! Our first cookbook, which had four different publishers and four different titles like *Cooking Around The World*, and *If Kalimos Had A Chef*. This one has our Nutty Maple recipe (called Nutty Maple Molasses in the book). One of my brothers found a used copy for 39 cents on Amazon.

Eat Well Be Happy: A Second Bite (our second cookbook) has the other four: Chocolate Berry, Maple Almond, Maple Raspberry Blueberry and Peanut Chocolate.

For almond lovers. For maple syrup lovers. For grain lovers. Allergies? Feel free to substitute one grain for another. If you want to use only oats, go for it, although I like variety and believe each grain brings something different to the table. Yes, use only organic grains. It's that important.

Years ago, we started making our granola with a non-GMO canola oil. (And no, canola oil is not poisonous). Today, our kitchen prefers sunflower oil.

As most of you know, we made our Maple Almond granola in a not-so-sweet version, just for our shop. The recipe is the same except that you use half the amount of maple syrup.

The original recipe called for desiccated coconut, and you'll see that here. In fact, we took out the coconut for commercial production. You can take it out, too, if you like.

Stark Sisters Maple Almond Granola

Makes 12 servings

½ C dried unsweetened coconut	1 C barley flakes
3 C sliced almonds	1 C maple syrup
2 C rolled oats	¼ C canola or sunflower oil
1 C wheat flakes	1 tsp real vanilla extract
1 C rye flakes	¼ tsp good salt

Preheat oven to 300 degrees.

Mix dry ingredients except salt in a large bowl. (If you don't have a large enough bowl, divide between 2 bowls. For example, 1 cup oats in 1 bowl, and 1 cup in a second bowl).

Pour wet ingredients over dry and mix well using your hands or a rubber spatula. Add salt and mix again. Make sure all grains are well-coated.

Spread granola in shallow pans and bake until golden brown and dry, about 1½ hours. Stir gently every 15-20 minutes. Baking times varies due to weather, the size of your pans, and your oven.

When granola is dry and golden brown, remove from oven and stir. Let cool completely before storing in airtight containers.

• •

In the beginning, when we roasted granola in our one oven in the shop, right back in our kitchen, people would come back, and our granola never got a chance to cool because people refused to wait until it did. "Just give me a pound in a soup container, no lid necessary," they would plead.

Ah, memories. Now it's time for new ones. Let us know when you make your own Stark Sisters Granola at home.

I'd like to end by saying that our customers did not go quietly into the night. Some tried to persuade us to re-open, to keep making Stark Sisters. Some wrote me passionate notes. I love this back and forth with Tom Miller when we let our Nutty Maple flavor go a few months before we closed down the company altogether.

From: Tom, **Sent:** Sunday, May 27, 2018 2:45 PM

Dear Stark Sisters, The word "addiction" inadequately describes my relationship with your Nutty Maple Granola. It is the beautiful crunchy start of my day that propels me out of bed each morning.

So, imagine my horror when, frighteningly low, I found your store out of this product just before this long weekend.

I vowed, then and there, to never let this happen again.

Therefore, I would like to come in and purchase at least ten pounds as soon as it is available. I live in Concord and so will just come in and pick it up when you have it back in stock. But, please hurry. My present foul mood will persist, my wife is not speaking to me, and even the dog is avoiding me until I can again start my day with a bowl of Stark Sisters Nutty Maple Granola. I sincerely hope that you are making a large batch just now. My marriage and a small frightened dog depend on it. Your humble servant, Tom Miller.

From: Debra (that's me!) **Sent:** Monday, May 28, 2018 7:19 AM

Oh, Tom. We struggled long and hard and finally had to stop making Stark Sisters Nutty Maple Granola. Our co-packer could make no less than a batch, which was many, many more cases that we could sell before it spoiled, and the last few times, we gave away way many cases to soup kitchens in order that it not be wasted.

Our Maple Almond and Maple Raspberry Blueberry are still in distribution with United Natural Foods, which means many mouths eat those flavors. Nutty Maple was always my favorite, but the market didn't agree.

You are hilarious. I hope your wife is laughing as hard as I am.

From: Tom, **Sent:** Monday, May 28, 2018 7:37 AM

It is with a heavy heart that I acknowledge the untimely demise of the Nutty Maple. I have purchased and this morning consumed a bowl of your Maple Almond, but, while good, it is just not the same.

If you could send me the bulk recipe for Nutty Maple, I can most likely calculate the smaller quantities myself (I have to put my MIT degree to good use sometime) unless the reduced quantity changes the ratio of ingredients. I will definitely give it a try, but I fear that I may be unable to achieve the perfection that was uniquely yours.

Thank you so much for your response. And, if you see a short, myopic, balding, past middle-aged man slouching sorrowfully through your store in West Concord holding a basket of ingredients for Nutty Maple, please say hello so that I can thank you for this kind response in person. All the best, Tom.

Chapter 12

Cookbooks And "Eat Well Be Happy," The TV Show

Our shop has published three cookbooks, all of which led, in the normal course of events, to *Eat Well Be Happy*, the public access television show. These projects were part of my "let's simplify life. Let's slow down and smell the roses" plan. When my family asked what the heck, my response was always that everything was connected to food, community and health. I wasn't really adding anything new at all to my plate.

Ahem. Who was correct? I was wrong, of course. Way wrong, but still moving forward. Take the fact I am eager today to talk to sponsors for *Eat Well Be Happy*. Take this book, for instance!

But what's it like, you ask, to write cookbooks? I'd be lying if I said it's a delight. If you're planning to write one, the only advice I can give is to gird your loins. It's a long haul. If you do the job right, you'll chop carrots, make soup, chop more carrots and make the same soup again, and then again, to make sure the recipe is copacetic. You'll write down every small step, except, perhaps, how to peel an onion.

You can't assume your reader knows anything, except, you hope, how to peel that onion. But most everything has to be spelled out and the instructions easy to follow. The flip side is that you have to realize you're not the expert, that there are plenty of cooks who can dance circles around you while throwing knives in the air. You're not the juggler supreme. After you've got your hundreds of recipes, you have to put your rear end in a chair and type everything up: ingredients, measurements, text, instructions, notes and any other step along the way. Then you give those recipes to someone to test. In my case, my friend and co-worker, Mary Kadlik, was my go-to person. If she liked the recipe, thought it was easy to follow, and turned out like something the hubby would adore, we'd high-five and put a check at the top of the page.

There were times Mary sent me back to my stove and back to the computer. I repeated my tasks until Mary was satisfied.

Once your recipes are set and you've got them all typed up, (and if you're as lucky as I was), either you have a real publisher who then takes the book off your hands (books one and two) or you happen to have a brother like David Stark, who takes everything off your plate (book two after the publisher vamoosed, and book three). Your brother chooses style, font, performs formatting magic with cookbook software and shazam! You've got a cookbook ready to send to a Print-On-Demand house like Lightning Source.

Our first cookbook had several real publishers. It has one today. While a publisher takes everything off your to-do list, you also have no say in the matter of the cover, the font, the book size or anything. A publisher pays for everything and expects you, if you're not a famous person, to market yourself so they can recoup their investment. I didn't know how to market myself or the books. I didn't have a "platform" of fans. None of my publishers, starting with Keats Publishing and ending with VanderWyk and Burnham, got rich. I don't know if they even made their investment back.

Writing a cookbook definitely doesn't guarantee fame and fortune for either the cookbook author or the publisher. There are some lucky few, and you might be one of those. But to the question, "Can I quit my day job once my book is out there?" my answer is, "Don't you wish!"

So why write a cookbook in the first place?

In my case, it's because I wanted to get people back into their kitchens. I wanted my simple-to-make, homey recipes to inspire and delight. I wanted folks to make my dishes and bring them to the table to share with family and friends. That was, and remains, my mission. One that I'm passionate about.

Folks tell me all the time how they are back in their kitchens, feeling happy. They tell me our books have led to dinner parties and impromptu get-togethers. That they make holidays less stressful. Mission: Accomplished, and anything beyond that is pure gravy. Our cookbooks are:

- ***If Kallimos Had A Chef* (by publisher VanderWyk and Burnham, thanks to my friend Meredith Rutter who put a novel spin on the original book published by Keats Publishing)**

- ***Eat Well Be Happy, A Second Bite***

- ***Blue Ribbon Edition, From Our Kitchen To Yours***

Each of our store newsletters contains a new recipe, and by now we have more than enough material for another book. But should a fourth cookbook ever see the light of day, it would definitely be because someone else's rear end sat in a chair.

And should any of our cookbooks go out of print, know that our other brother, Daniel Stark, the youngest, lost his copy of our first cookbook and was able to get it on Amazon for 39 cents (plus $3.95 for shipping). When the book arrived, it was signed by me, which he thought was a hoot, but which proves my point that cookbooks are not a guarantee that you'll ever be able to buy a car like an antique Thunderbird, if that's your style.

One of my favorite recipes from our first cookbook is "Quinoa with Pine Nuts and Apricots." We also made it on our cooking show. This is one of the most requested dishes in our shop's kitchen, and it's a dish I bring to potlucks. Nowadays, we make this with roasted, salted shelled pistachios because the price of pine nuts has gone through the roof. Organic shelled pistachios are not cheap either, and you could use pumpkinseeds or sunflower seeds if paying the mortgage is more important.

Quinoa is one of the three grains that's a complete protein. It sprouts when it cooks. Its mild buttery flavor and soft texture takes on whatever personality you choose to give it, and this personality is a winner!

If you're entertaining kids and want something interactive, prepare the grain with the dressing and then set out an assortment of ingredients to mix in (raisins, dates, all kinds of veggies...) Kids really love making the dish their own.

Quinoa with Pine Nuts and Apricots

Serves 8

4 C water	1 tsp ground coriander
2 C quinoa	2 tsp ground cumin
1 C toasted pine nuts*	2 tsp sea salt
1 C dried apricots	2 tsp paprika
2 Tbsp fresh lemon juice	1 bunch scallions, thinly sliced, or
4 Tbsp extra virgin olive oil	1 bunch parsley, chopped

In a medium saucepan, bring water to a boil. Stir in quinoa, cover pot, simmer for 15 minutes. Turn off flame and let pot sit covered for a bit.

In the meantime, toast pine nuts by stirring in a dry frying pan until they become aromatic and toasty–don't burn–the process just takes a minute. If using roasted, salted, shelled pistachios, you don't need to roast them anymore in a frying pan or anywhere else. You save your-self some labor and money!

In a large mixing bowl, combine dressing of lemon juice, olive oil, cori-ander, cumin, paprika and salt. Use a rubber spatula to combine. Turn quinoa into the mixing bowl. Toss gently using that rubber spatula. Grain is warm and tender, so don't use a wooden or metal spoon which will crush grain. Fluff grain from time to time. When quinoa is almost room temp, add pine nuts (or pistachios) and dried fruit. Mix in pars-ley and/or scallions when completely cool. Serve at room temperature, because that's how it tastes best.

My advice: substitute roasted, salted, pistachio nut meats–meaning the shells have already been removed for you–for pine nuts, just because of price. We sell pistachio meats in our store, and I'm sure you can get them elsewhere, too.

• •

Eat Well Be Happy was produced in my home kitchen, and it was great fun sharing the "spotlight" with the amazing and talented crew from our kitchen at Debra's Natural Gourmet. We were lucky to work with Acton TV, a public access TV station in Acton, where I live. The crew came to my home most months for close to three years, and each time they came, we shot four shows, one right after the other. My goal was always to start filming, cameras and sound rolling, at 9:00 and finish the last show and the last recipe by noon-ish so we all (TV crew, cooks and guests) could sit down and eat lunch together at a reasonable time. Mostly, we sat down about 1:00, but it was always a feast!

We got to *show* everyone how easy it is to make dishes, and we called out by name some of favorite products like Bragg's organic apple cider vinegar and Eden beans. We loved talking about why Eden, why Nutiva coconut oil and why grass-fed dairy, why only grass-fed meats. We talked about extra virgin olive oils and salts like Celtic, Himalayan and Real Salt.

At this writing, *Eat Well Be Happy* has had 80 episodes. Though we've not filmed any new ones in more than two years, we're still the second most downloaded show on public access TV. Stations around the country call and beg for more shows–which means there's a hunger for something that was produced and shot in my home kitchen. Just recently I got a call from a station in Maryland, excitedly telling me we'd won an award, and this after no production of any new episodes in three years!

Like our cookbooks, that show is a labor of love. A ton of work for no pay and definitely not a get-rich-quick scheme.

I chose recipes, I typed the scripts. I cleaned the house, did the shopping, the dragging everything home and up the stairs to my kitchen. My friend, Roxanne Bispham, aka our terrific kitchen manager, would arrive at my home the day before and help me do prep for the shows. She was my moral support. We organized pots, pans and plates for each recipe and each show. We placed spoons and knives, and measuring cups at the ready, too. We organized everything that would be used per recipe and per show.

If an apple pie was part of a show, we had to make one the day before so it could be swapped out the next day with the pie on air that had just gone into the oven. We had to have an apple pie that we could sniff to show the camera, steaming and fully baked. We roasted a chicken the day before to swap-out the next day, too. We made soup and stew ahead. Our swap-outs were for any dish that needed to bake or roast or stew for longer than 10-15 minutes. We needed to be able to do an abracadabra for people to see the dish, done.

Without counting swap outs, we were prepping four recipes per 30-minute episode for four episodes, which mean 16 total dishes. Now add in the swap outs. That's a lot of food.

Along with Roxanne, Acton TV and Mike Chapman were in my home the day before as well to set up the cameras and lights and sound systems. Everything was left ready to rock and roll for the next day. Mike's job was sound and editing, so our shows could put their best foot forward. Brudder David came up a couple of times and lent a hand. Mostly he told me to be myself, to lean into the camera, to think of the camera as a best friend to whom I was talking. I get that now. I didn't quite, then.

Mary G. arrived the morning of to do our makeup. And during all the busyness, and even though I was on camera the whole time, I ran around like a chicken with my head cut off, because I was responsible for everything and everyone. I needed an assistant so I could calm down.

Even Roxanne and our kitchen staff, who were my co-conspirators and guests, weren't able to just enjoy. They flew in and out because they were all needed back in the store's kitchen to make the hot meal or get a catering job out the door.

After everyone left my house, I was IN the kitchen for hours of dishwashing and washing floors. My dark secret: I would often collapse on the sofa and eat two pints of ice cream. It would take me days to restore my home to peace and quiet.

It was intense. Our staff didn't get paid anything extra, and I needed a shopper, a chopper, a dishwasher and an assistant, as well as someone to do marketing and publicity.

Yes, we all dream of filming again. We'd like to up our game. You bet your bippee. Half the folks in this country love watch cooking shows, and if I do say so myself, *Eat Well Be Happy* entertains. Our shows, again in my humble opinion, have both a light touch and sense of humor. Remember the time Roxanne saved my bacon when my waffles wouldn't come out of the waffle iron, so she spontaneously turned them into the ever-and-still popular waffle bites? Or the time I caused flames to shoot to the ceiling when making blintz shells?

The following recipe has been featured in our newsletter, and we made it on the show—and of course we serve it in the store. It's inspired by The Life-Changing Loaf of Bread by Sarah Briton, and I want to give her a big thumbs up here. My adaptation changes it from a bread to a crispy cracker; I changed some of the ingredients, added more seeds, and simplified the process so I knew that I would actually make it! The result, like Sarah's bread, is chock-a-block full of nutrients: protein, minerals, fiber and gluten-free, nut-free and vegan if you use coconut oil (or olive or sesame oil; both are options). We love it, and you will too. Should you use organic seeds and oats? Goes without saying.

Last I heard, we were making 3,000 boxes of Change-Your-Life Crisps each month!

Change-Your-Life Crisps

Makes about 15 crackers

1 C hulled sunflower seeds	4 Tbsp psyllium seed husks
½ C whole flax seeds	1 tsp good salt

½ C hulled pumpkin seeds	3 Tbsp melted coconut oil or ghee
1 ½ C thick rolled oats	2 C water
2 Tbsp chia seeds	

In a bowl, combine all ingredients, stirring well. Let the dough stand for about 5 minutes; then, using a small size scoop or a ¼ C measuring cup, dollop crackers onto greased cookie sheet(s). Flatten with a wet hand. (I like to flatten my bread thin because I like it crisp and crunchy when I eat it.) You can make these perfectly round or not, it's up to you.

Sarah says to let her bread sit at room temp at least 2 hours, all day, or overnight. I have found letting my slices or disks–I'm not sure what to call them!–sit about 20 minutes works for this version.

Preheat oven to 325. Bake bread 20 minutes. Flip and bake about another 20 minutes, depending upon how crisp you like your bread, your oven, the weather and your baking pans (they're all different).

These freeze beautifully but also last at room temperature on an uncovered plate for a few days. I love having a few slices as breakfast with warm tea and a piece of fruit.

Having a dinner party? Make tiny cracker-sized breads and put them out with guacamole or hummus.

• •

So, if you're Subaru or Viking River Cruises and want to help us make people laugh more in their kitchens, give us a call. If you want to interview us on *Good Morning America* ("Cooking show sensation!" GMA would exclaim), call the store at 978-371-7573 and ask for Debra. If you're a company in the natural products industry whose products we use with gay abandon, also call us. We won't bite.

Until then, our show can be found on our store's website, www.DebrasNaturalGourmet.com, some websites of independent natural food stores around the country and on public access stations around the country.

I love one caller who said, "You changed my life! Your immune-boosting soup kept me and my family from getting sick this winter." Another who said, "You made me laugh so hard that I almost choked until I decided it was safer to spray my family with smoothie out my nose and mouth."

Chapter 13

Our Industry And INFRA-Ites!

I am always amazed how eager customers in our shop are for information about the natural products industry and about our brother and sister independents around the country. Our customers want to know the inside scoop. They want a glimpse behind the scenes. They want a bird's eye view of Natural Products Expo East and West.

Nowadays Expo West has more than 3,500 exhibitors from all over the world and more than 89,000 attendees. East, a more intimate show, had "only" 1,500 exhibits and 29,000 attendees in 2019. Imagine halls on four levels with huge escalators going up and down. Imagine watching New Hope Natural Media's Pitch Slam (our version of the Shark Tank). New Hope are the folks who put on our trade shows and publish one of our trade magazines, *Natural Foods Merchandiser*. They are terrific!

Rick Antonelli has worn many hats. When he was VP of Cornucopia (a major distributor now known as UNFI) he was famous for throwing parties at Expos to thank retailers for their business and support. One of the nibbles provided was always shrimp. Said Rick, "My God. With all the vegetarians and vegans in our industry, I've never seen shrimp disappear so fast. It got so that each year I'd order a truckload of shrimp. It was never enough!"

Another story (no one will confirm this one) is that our herbalists who attended trade shows would always find a place to go skinny-dipping. And another rumor has it that our folks party harder than any other industry at any other convention.

Not our crew, the staff from Debra's. We even make it to morning walks and yoga outside in front of the hall to Natural Products Expo West. There's no dirt to dish on our crew!

Well, I suppose that's not completely true. There is the time that David Abbott came down with the Norovirus infection in Anaheim, California, far from home.

As you know, this virus is highly contagious with sudden onset of severe symptoms that are awful. David was sharing a hotel room with Adam, who ended up sleeping in the hotel lobby (there were no more rooms available). On different flights going home, half the folks on David's plane were also returning from Expo West. Those folks, to this day, remind us that one of ours did them in. That thanks to David, nearly half the natural products industry living and working near Boston were nearly wiped out! Pat from Common Crow in Gloucester, with whom we'd had dinner two nights earlier, didn't even make it on the plane. She sent us a picture of herself wearing a wool hat and big sweatshirt, which she'd had to buy in sunny CA because she was shivering and so sick.

When we attend these expos, we come home jazzed up (if we're still healthy, that is). When we're in Baltimore or Anaheim, or whatever city the expo is in, we realize we're not alone. Our companies, our distributors and other stores all share the same passion—to change the world one bite at a time. We are reminded that what we do is different from, say, selling shoes.

Let me state for the record: I love shoes. I wear them. I relish forays into shoe stores. I can talk about rubber soles and arch support. Slingbacks.

But when we're at these shows, we realize with sudden, startling clarity how we're different. Can you imagine, for instance, employees who work at CVS or Publix knowing that formaldehyde in Mr. Clean Magic Erasers is flat out dangerous? I would eat my hat if Home Depot suddenly stopped selling Monsanto's/Bayer's weedkilling product, Roundup, just because studies link it to cancer. Nor can I picture conversations in the aisles of Stop 'n Shop about inflammation. Or why shampoos and conditioners are safer if they don't contain Polyethylene Glycol (PEG).

Our industry *is* different. As an industry, we've been around since the 1920's, when in response to the introduction of synthetic fertilizers and pesticides, a group of farmers came together and founded an organic and biodynamic food movement, which led to our trade association, formed in 1953, that worked to connect buyers and sellers of organic foods.

Our industry is the reason McD and the crowd under the yellow arch are now committed to removing preservatives from their American cheese, Big Mac special sauce and pickle slices. (But order anything with eggs at fast food restaurants and you still get a "premium egg blend," which includes propylene glycol, also found in antifreeze; butylhydroquinone, used in varnish; and calcium silicate, used as a sealant for roads. "Premium egg blend" is not good old eggs!)

Our industry works hard to educate, and I love Dr. Joel Furhman of PBS fame who says we can prevent disease by eating a nutrient-dense diet. Instead of detecting disease with, say, a mammogram, Dr. Furhman recommends preventing disease in the first place with organic food. Instead of eating 62 percent of our calories from nutrient-deficient processed foods and sweets, he urges us to switch to a G-BOMBS diet–greens, beans, onions, mushrooms, berries, seeds–all sourced organically, of course.

I grin at the saying, "The whiter the bread, the sooner you're dead." And I resonate with Joel's statement that we have weapons of mass destruction on every corner–Dunkin' Donuts!–which leads to the stat that 18 cents out of every dollar spent in this country is spent managing disease that might be prevented with some changes in our diet.

These issues, and more, are what inform our industry's behavior. However, within the natural products industry, the large chains like Whole Foods, known as the supernaturals, bring big money and clout, and they negotiate contracts with distributors and companies that put independent stores like ours at risk. The playing field is simply not level.

Thank you to all who vote with their dollars by coming through our doors. Thank you to everyone who tells us that they want us to thrive, to always be a part of their community.

That's when I tell these folks about a trade association called The Independent Natural Food Retailers Association (INFRA). INFRA is, like buying our building, one of the best things that happened to us. I often wonder if we'd be here today without them.

Founded in 2004, today this organization comprises more than 225 collective stores with 350 locations, with more stores asking to join every day. We have a national purchasing agreement with a major distributor, KeHe, that helps us compete with Trader Joes, Target, Kroeger and all the big chains.

But INFRA also brings our stores together, creating a far-flung community so we can chuckle at the chipmunk brought in by a shopper as a service animal, or cry when one of us is grieving because flood waters swept their store away. We meet in what are called "sharegroups," hosted by different member stores. Sharegroups talk about leadership training, succession planning and how to make sure our kitchens are successful. All this support and networking keeps the wow factor in our shops alive. We have our own trade show and annual INFRA conference, which Roxanne, our kitchen manager, says feels like going home to visit family.

But it's the conversations on the listserv that are my favorite. What is a listserv? It's simply a closed group on the internet that allows emails to go back and forth. Member stores send out questions on all kinds of topics, and responses come from around the country in quick order. Reading the emails often sparks conversation, just like the conversations we have in our shop with our customers.

One conversation I enjoyed was about the Keto diet:

Pam, Good Natured Market and Vegetarian Café, Martinsburg, WV, wrote: "Hi, all. How are you dealing with the Keto diet? My state of West Virginia has one of the highest obesity rates in the country. How can we navigate this no-carb lifestyle in a vegetarian-based cafe and market?

"I don't agree with the dietary constraints or the long-term viability of the Keto lifestyle. Monk fruit, xylitol and erythritol sugars, psyllium husk as a flour substitute, how can that be good? Sweets seem to be the driving force. I want to promote health."

Brian Mosser, Get Healthy, Brooksville & Spring Hill, FL, wrote Pam: "Hi Pam, I guess this as an opportunity to start conversations and educate customers.

"We have a café in our store and one of our employees is following the Keto lifestyle, as a vegan, and having great results. She shares her story with customers, and she has been tweaking some of our menu items to make them friendlier to the Keto diet....

"I personally think the 'natural' sweeteners are much better for people than white sugar or high fructose corn syrup."

To which **Pam** responded: "I would much rather sell folks purple cauliflower, kiwi berries and local heirloom tomatoes. A customer will spend $14 on two bags of stevia-based chocolate chips and then walk right past the organic produce. In the end they are not changing their diet, the craving for fats and sweets still controls what they eat.

"Comfort foods are part of our food culture and I am not in disagreement here about the value of sugar alcohols, etc. I do talk to folks; I just worry that we are creating a false narrative. Treats are not the basis of a good diet. Bacon and butter in excess cannot be a good thing.

"My customers are telling me that their desire for 'a sweet thing' is overwhelming. This diet seems to perpetuate that need—most beans, fruits and whole grains are not on the table. Is this good? I don't know."

John H. Wood II, The Green Grocer, Portsmouth, RI, wrote: "I was thinking while reading this that these dietary trends always seem to exclude elements of a whole foods diet. The Keto and the gluten-free trends exclude primary sources of fiber…and can be devoid of fiber completely.

"I am trying to promote the idea of 'slow carb' in our prepared foods section. With signage reading *Low Carb? Think Slow Carb*, we are starting a conversation around why fiber-rich diets (notice diet, not supplements) are better for weight loss, cardiovascular health, nourishing healthy gut bacteria and are a critical element in the treatment of diabetes. Americans are consuming on average only about 20-30 percent of their recommended fiber intake. Lack of fiber has a strong correlation to increased disease.

"This thoughtful discourse is refreshing in what seems to be an otherwise controversial world."

David, City Feed and Supply, Jamaica Plain, MA. ended this thread with: "*Slow Carb*! Great idea and great points."

Today Adam sits on the INFRA board, which is one way we give back to this group. Through INFRA we've met people like Terry Brett and his family from Pennsylvania. We've visited and traded recipes with the fine folks at Jimbo's in California. We're impressed by John H. Wood II of The Green Grocer, Portsmouth, Rhode Island, and Joe Hamilton, Pilgrim's Market, Coeur d'Alene, Idaho. We have adopted things we learned from John Pittari of New Morning, in Connecticut.

We whoop at (or cry with) our western counterparts, some of whose customers wear their guns into the store. We go gaga over stores who added organic farms and school education programs. It's wonderful to know that other stores, too, bring people together in community.

We've gotten to know Laughing Water whose store, Real Food Market and Deli, is in Montana. Fellow INFRA store Bi-Rite in the San Francisco area amazes us. They have more daily customers per square foot in their tiny store than any shop in the country! Martindale's is the oldest natural food store in the country, and The Turnip Truck has grown to be the largest in TN.

There are small stores like Bath Natural Market in Maine, and large ones such as Alfalfa's in Colorado. We have stores with multiple locations like Big Bear Natural Foods in New Jersey, and single stores like Brighter Day in Savannah, and Nuts 'n Berries Healthy Market, in Brookhaven, Georgia. Becky and Michael's store, Pangaea Naturals, Manahawkin, New Jersey, has to win the prize for best-dressed owners, both hipster and Hawaiian style.

We're honored to be among the ten Massachusetts stores who are all INFRA members: Cambridge Naturals, City Feed and Supply, Common Crow Natural Market, Cornucopia Natural Wellness Market, Down to Earth Natural Foods, Guido's Fresh Marketplace, Nantucket Green Grocer, Roots Natural Foods and Rory's Market.

In our region, Pat Rector, who was with New Morning Natural Foods in Woodbury, Connecticut before becoming an INFRA staffer, comes to visit and work with us periodically. Pat's title is Region Manager, but we call her "the fixer!" She's tough and wants us to know our numbers and think about our personal goals. She challenges those of us who are "older" to think about how we're going to pass on the stuff that may be only in our heads. She reminds us that we're all always in training. "Think of it like you signed up for a triathlon. What would you need to do to prepare?" she asks.

I thought you might enjoy stories shared by a handful of INFRA-ites. Here's another peek behind the curtain.

In no particular order...

Jeremy from Hawthorne Valley Farm in upstate New York: A few years ago, I fielded a call about our yogurt. Apparently, a woman was suffering from a severe yeast infection and wanted to apply Hawthorne Valley yogurt directly to the infected location. Yogurt contains a lot of probiotics, but I'm a guy, and I'd never had to consider using yogurt in this way. I told her I thought it was okay. I suggested checking in with her doctor. I don't remember much of the conversation after she described the very specific turkey baster she planned to use, and how. I don't have the same relationship to yogurt as I did before.

Billy Griffin, New Moon Natural Foods, North Tahoe-Truckee area of California: Many years ago, we expanded our store by taking over the adjacent unit. As part of the remodel, we prepped the new unit, then moved our store into it while we remodeled the old one. We did the switch-over in one night. The following day we directed customers to the entry door of the new unit. Knowing this would cause confusion, I had a two-by-three foot sign printed on a foam core with four-inch letters reading "What's Going on Here?" and a bullet point explanation of the project below. I placed the sign on an easel six inches inside the doorway, so customers would have to literally walk around it to get inside. In the first three days, I counted TWELVE instances in which someone navigated the easel, surveyed the new store and, with no trace of irony, uttered the words, What's going on here?"

Jane Pittari, New Morning in Woodbury, Connecticut: Years ago, I had a woman ask me for nut crackers, so I took her to the shelf and pointed out the Blue Diamond nut crackers. We went back and forth between "No, I want nut crackers!" and "These ARE nut crackers!" Of course, what she wanted was the utensil to crack nuts. I think I might have found that funnier than she did, but I took her to the housewares section, and she got what she needed.

Tina, Royal River Natural Foods, Freeport, Maine: Many years ago, I was ringing out a woman who was purchasing about 20 tubes of Arnica. She said, "I bet you're wondering why I'm buying so much." I said, "Oh no, it's a good to keep Arnica on hand." In her exact words she said, "I am getting a boob job, I have always wanted bigger boobies." I didn't know what to say. Luckily, she started laughing and so did I. We laughed at the counter for quite a few minutes and then she was on her way.

Kevin Hamm, Free Market in Appleton Wisconsin: I had a woman come in and ask for grass-fed chicken. I tried to find out why she was requesting chicken that was grass-fed (those of you who have grown up on farms can verify that chickens don't graze on grass!) She informed me she was vegan. She figured if the chicken only ate plants, she could eat it. I tried to explain but she informed me that she couldn't believe we didn't have grass-fed chicken, and she would just go to Trader Joe's instead.

Sander Habraken, Meadow Farm Foods, Fergus Falls, Minnesota: We had a gentleman come in asking where we kept the great prepared meals in a can. This caused head-scratching because it didn't seem like a product we would have on the shelf. He described it in detail and said we just started stocking it and that it was delicious. The staff was a bit startled because the description did match one newer product very well. Our new line of apparently poorly-labeled organic dog food. From then on, we proudly sold that product as being tried and tested.

Sheila Ouellette, New Morning Natural Foods, Biddeford and Kennebunk, Maine: The workday was over, and my husband Paul was here to pick me up. He parked in front with our big old hand-me-down Pontiac. I walked out of the door, placed the bag of groceries into the back seat, and turned back to lock the door. We drove home. The phone rings...it's the local police department saying someone was locked in our store! Apparently when I was placing my groceries into the back seat just before locking up, a customer walked in. He proceeded to the freezer to purchase an ice cream bar, went to the check out and realized he was alone. He then noticed the lights were out. He checked the door...it was locked. (This was an old building, you could only lock it from the outside). He sat on the floor and ate his ice cream. He noticed a pay phone (that was all we had back then!) and called the police. He was from out of town ... Paul gave him a ride to the beach and apologized.

Jamie Gass of the Organic Food Depot, Norfolk, Virginia: I still find this story funny. Customer came in looking for suntan lotion without any SPF (Debra here: As you know, SPF stands for "sun protection factor," a measure of how long a sunscreen will protect you from ultraviolet B rays). She said she was allergic to SPFs. I asked if there was a particular ingredient or ingredients she was trying to avoid, but she insisted it was the SPFs. I could not help this customer.

Edward Blanton, Health Trail Natural Foods, Newport News, Virginia: Perhaps in his grief he was not aware of the what he said or how it sounded, but someone called our store to say, "My Uncle Joe died last week, do you have anything for that." Pause. I waited for the cause of death like heart attack, cancer, etc. Finally, I asked, "What did he die of sir?" And then he said, "I don't know, you know...death."

Mystery Store: (I can't tell you who told me this story or where he or she lives. West coast, east coast, mountains or ocean. I promised not to spill the beans). For the last three years I have gone to the supermarket and bought about a $1,000 worth of matzo for Passover. I take it back to our store. Why? Well, the markets have a great selection and the retail price is cheaper than any wholesale price I've seen from any distributor. Our distributors, UNFI and KEHE, advertise Passover programs with a regular suggested retail price of $5.99. Preorder and save 10 percent!!! I guarantee the matzo will be out of stock and we will never get any. Meanwhile our supermarkets have pallet displays in the center of the store selling boxes of matzo for $2.99 a box. When I'm in line, the hardest part is explaining to the Jewish people in line behind me why I'm buying it all. They assume I am hosting some super-duper Passover party. I do get some dark joy in the hope that I wipe the markets out of organic matzo so it will be available only at our shop the last couple days of Passover!

Another anonymous report from a Pennsylvania store: So this teen-something comes up to our customer service earlier today and asks if we have anything to help her pass a drug test that her mom is making her take. She was in the store with her mother, by the way. We tell her we don't sell that kind of product. Five minutes later she comes back and asks the same staffer for a job application. Maybe she's been dating the 18-year-old who was recently arrested for attempted carjacking. He could only be charged with attempt because after forcing the driver out of the car and getting in, he discovered that the car was a stick shift which he did not know how to drive. He was arrested moments after getting out of the car.

Sam Mogannam of Bi-Rite in San Francisco: Our mission is "creating community through food." We draw this as an equilateral triangle. The points are our guests, our staff and our producers. It doesn't matter which way you turn the triangle; no one point is more important or weighted, each is interdependent on the other for success. We can't have a strong relationship with guests unless we have good relationships with our vendors and are able to secure really good food to sell. And if we don't have this food to sell, then we don't make money to pay our staff to provide them with meals and benefits. It's all linked, and it all must be treated equally. The fourth component is that we draw a circle around the triangle and that's our environment, the earth. It's more than putting a tomato in someone's basket; it's about building a community and a strong local economy."

Jarred Gild, Western Market, Ferndale, Michigan: I had a customer sent in by his wife for "umami." I proceeded to longwindedly explain the concept of umami and foods that can impart umami flavor like aged cheese, fermented foods, fish sauce, sea greens, etc. But he insisted it was a thing, like one thing, that you just buy...we both left the interaction a little confused. A few months later I was at Trader Joe's, and what do they sell? A tube, labeled UMAMI. "A potent mix of tomato paste, miso, anchovies and more."

Jarred goes on to say, "We also like to insert the occasional pop culture reference into the signage. Credit for the best pun goes to my brother, who made a Die Hard sign for the snack set that had a picture of John McClane (in front of an explosion, of course) that just said CHIPEE KI-YAY MOTHERCRUNCHERS. The most enduring though is the first one I made, an obscure reference to the show SEALAB 2021 that just replaces the name of the store with Mousebrain, with the line, "We'll need cheese for the voyage, mostly parmesans and romanos. Hard Cheeses for a hard journey," and the picture below. A very thin slice of people shopping for cheese that watched surreal late-night cartoons in 2001 get it, but they go bananas when they see it.

I'd like to circle back to our industry and what it stands for. We sell many products that are organic. Small organic producers celebrate inconsistencies in handmade cheese and apple pies. But modern food giants like Heinz often scratch their heads. They have difficulty making every jar of Heinz organic ketchup taste the same or even sourcing enough organic tomatoes.

For a sense of why Big Business and the natural products industry and organics often don't mix, it helps to visit Jack and Anne Lazor of Butterworks Farm who have been producing organic yogurt in Vermont since 1975. Their 45 milking cows are raised from birth and have names like Peaches and Moonlight. All of the food for the cows—and most of what the Lazors eat, too—comes from the farm, and Anne keeps their charges healthy with a mix of homeopathic medicines and nutritional supplements. Butterworks produces 9,000 quarts of yogurt a week, and no one can pressure them to make more. When consumers buy organic in our shop, they are voting for the Butterworks ethic. They don't quite trust organics being produced by Clorox or General Mills.

Chapter 14

Favorite Newsletter Columns And Other Thoughts

Since I don't think God is doing a very good job teaching us how to take care of ourselves, I've stepped into the breach. That's what I do in the shop. I delight in sharing small bites of information. I call these health tidbits. On the other hand, our monthly newsletters are conversations we have with our customers about all manner of health topics —just more in depth than my tidbits.

Because we write those articles ourselves, from the front lines, they mirror questions we get asked. "I have trouble sleeping," many folks say, and beg for advice. "My college kid is almost paralyzed with anxiety, and I wonder if there's something natural they could try?" confide others. Surprisingly, many people reluctant to use prescription drugs with side-effects come in about toenail fungus.

We write about subjects that are of concern to many people. That means an article about how to get your parakeet's feathers shinier probably won't fly.

Adam writes better articles than I do. I'm the family crank. The articles I write make me feel like Don Quixote, off tilting at windmills and various causes about which I'm passionate. And I like the sentence, "Build it and they will come!" and envision folks going "Ah-hah!" because of something I write.

Sometimes I hit a bull's eye, and our customers hug me. I get emails saying things like...

> Thank you for sharing this story publicly. I am finishing up my own letter, and tomorrow I plan to share your article on my social media accounts, asking others to add their voices. This is how I remain hopeful for change, instead of getting discouraged about the safety of our world. Together we CAN... thank you for leading the way.

According to our customers, articles in our monthly newsletter saved lives, made people guffaw and made them act and call Congress or write Tide's Proctor and Gamble.

We got a national boycott against Eden Foods called off. That article is on our store's website, if you want to read it. As a matter of fact, our website is where our newsletter articles reside. They make our website content-heavy and set us apart from other retail store websites. Our articles are heartfelt and the real deal. See for yourself at www.Debras-NaturalGourmet.com.

We write articles because a former Surgeon General said the Standard American Diet causes two million deaths a year. Statistics show that only nine percent of us are eating five servings of fruit and vegetables daily (and we're told we should be eating *more than* five servings anyway). What can we grab in the afternoon instead of that Snickers Bar?

But my tidbits aren't on our website, and I like tidbits because I have the attention span of a gnat. Some of you know this. I figure others may be in the same boat as I am. Tidbits are fun, and most of you know I always ask if folks are drinking enough water. Not cold water, I might add. "Sip hot water, or at least room temperature water because that's an old Ayurvedic remedy for whatever ails you. Sipping hot water throughout the day–every 15 minutes if you can–is said to settle the nervous system when one feels anxious."

Ayurveda, in case you're a newbie to this world of ours, is simply the ancient medicine of India.

In the dead of winter, or anytime you're not feeling like yourself, simplify what you eat. Don't sit down to a meal that has a thousand and one ingredients because digestion is hard work, and you want your body to work at boosting your immune system or fighting off that cold or flu instead of struggling with foie gras.

Another tidbit: The darker color a fruit, veggie or grain or bean is, the more antioxidants it has.

What are antioxidants? They're those substances that keep our cells from rusting prematurely. Think of a piece of iron that gets wet and rusts. Think of cutting a slice of apple and watching it turn brown when it sits on your kitchen counter exposed to air. Those are examples of oxidation. No way José do we want out cells to oxidize ahead of schedule. Of course, our cells naturally oxidize as we age, but they break down faster when we are stressed, breathe in polluted air, take medications, eat junk food and more.

We can protect ourselves if we eat foods that are high in antioxidants. Think dark leafy greens, berries, bright orange and purple yams, beets. Black beans, black rice.

The bright colors in candy corn and cherry soda don't count. Nor do those in processed American cheese slices.

Green tea and red tea are high in antioxidants. I once conducted a kitchen experiment. I brewed three pots of tea, one green, one red and one herbal. I left all the tea bags in each pot. I left the pots on my kitchen counter in the heat of summer. Within a couple of days, the pot of herbal tea was bubbling, fermenting and molding. The green and red teas stayed fresh as a daisy for over a week. Amazing! It was those antioxidants at work.

I espouse eating good fats because every cell, and that includes our brain cells, have to be coated with fat or those cells begin to dry out. Imagine your brain cells shriveling, dry and crusty because you're afraid to eat an avocado.

Here's a salad you can see us make on *Eat Well Be Happy*, our cooking show. Serve with ripe heirloom tomatoes and fish, chicken, tofu or beans. Did you know that chard, a member of the beet family, contains more than 13 antioxidants, and one of those, syringic acid, according to recent research, is good at regulating blood sugar? Another substance in chard, betalain, helps us detox.

Don't stint on avocados or good oils. This salad is meant to be luscious, and your body needs good fat.

Rainbow Chard Salad with Avocado

Serves 4 comfortably. Use organic ingredients, of course

1 bunch rainbow chard	1 tsp each good salt
2 cloves garlic, pressed	1 tsp ground black pepper
½ C extra virgin olive oil	1 C pitted niçoise olives*
1 Tbsp lemon juice + more to taste)	2-3 Hass avocados, peeled, cubed
1 tsp grated lemon zest	

Rinse chard and pat dry. Trim the stem ends, then slice stems and put in salad bowl. Lay 3 chard leaves on top of one another; roll them like a cigar. Slice thinly with a sharp knife. You can cut the long shreds in half to make it easier to eat. Put chard and remaining ingredients in salad bowl. Use 2 avocados if they are large, 3 if they are on the small side. Then toss with hands to combine everything well. Taste, adjust seasoning and enjoy. The chard salad without avocado keeps for days in the fridge. You could make it ahead and add avocado when you're ready to eat it.

Nicoise olives are flavorful but tiny, so you don't need to chop them Just make sure to buy them pitted, and we sell them that way. If you don't live near Concord, I bet you have a store that has pitted Nicoise olives, too.

• •

What are other good fats besides avocados? Oh, my goodness, so many! Think extra virgin olive oil, ghee, grass-fed butters, coconut oil, pumpkinseed oil and many more. Think nuts and seeds. Hemp seeds are outrageously high in fat that keeps us supple and our skin less wrinkled.

But everything in balance and harmony is a tidbit worth taking to heart. That means if you think tofu is God's gift to your health, don't eat it five times a day. More isn't always better or best. Back in the nineties, people thought if a little bit of soy (organic, Non-GMO) was good, eating it eight times daily would cure whatever ailed them. Why do we Americans think that if something is good for us, more will always allow us to walk on water and chew gum at the same time?

But enough of tidbits. To get more, come into the shop. Now we're onto some of my favorite newsletter articles in order of publication.

Healing with Aromatherapy, 2011

Members of a tribe in New Guinea say goodbye by putting a hand in each other's armpit then rubbing themselves with it, coating themselves with the other's scent. Similarly, in Elizabethan times a peeled apple was kept in a woman's armpit until it absorbed her odor, then given to her lover as a "love apple" so he could inhale her fragrance while they were apart. It is reported that Napoleon sent a message to Josephine: "Home in three days, don't wash."

Smell is our most primitive sense and directly accesses the hypothalamus, the gland which controls neurochemical and hormonal functions of the body. Smell can trigger memories, emotion, creativity and can help heal. This study of smell and how it affects us is called "aromatherapy," which uses essential oils distilled or extracted from flowers, trees, bushes and herbs.

It was the Egyptians who are generally recognized as the founders of aromatherapy. The Persians and ancient Arabs followed the recommendations of Hippocrates and used aromatic oils to purify the air and protect themselves from disease. In mediaeval Europe, plants like lavender, thyme and chamomile were used in meeting places and churches because when strewn underfoot and stepped on, they gave off scents, which had insecticidal and bactericidal properties, which helped counter the spread of infectious illness. They also deterred lice and fleas.

During the bubonic plague, grave robbers protected themselves by using a potion with garlic, rosemary, camphor, lavender, nutmeg, sage and cinnamon suspended in vinegar. In the 1930's French chemist, Rene M. Gattefosse, plunged his burned hand into a vat of lavender oil. The healing and calming effect this had gave birth in his studies to modern aromatherapy.

Today in Europe, aromatherapy is respected and used with other healing modalities because it helps the body heal itself on an emotional and physical level. The correct scent has been found to boost immunity, lower blood pressure, stimulate digestion and release endorphins (feel-good chemicals in the brain). Ain't that good to know!

Ancient writings tell us that cinnamon was sprinkled on beds before lovemaking. Today belief has it that cinnamon is an aphrodisiac for men. What's old is new, what's new is simply re-discovering the old.

If you want to try aromatherapy, start with oils whose scent you like. Read about that oil and you'll be surprised to find out that what you like is often what you need. You like what makes you feel good, what helps you achieve a goal or get through the day. For instance, clary sage, which I'm nuts about, is said to calm, sooth, re-establish equilibrium and induce a sense of euphoria. References also say that clary sage relieves mental fatigue and releases muscles. Bergamot is said to uplift and have a stabilizing effect on the emotions. It's often described as a ray of sunshine coming into one's life. Jasmine, nicknamed the "king" of oils, is said to open the heart and give a sense of relaxation. It's definitely a heavenly fragrance that for many instills confidence and inspires joy. Traditionally used as an aphrodisiac, jasmine is said to make one feel beautiful from within.

For insomnia, when my mind keeps going in circles, I've often found that sprinkling a few drops of marjoram essential oil together with a few drops of lavender either directly onto my pillow or into a diffuser really works. Sleep is deep and the worry resolves.

We all know that eucalyptus opens the sinuses. Lemon or orange or peppermint are said to make us feel more alert, lively and cheery. Lemon is used in some Japanese factories because it reportedly decreases sick days and increases productivity.

Lavender, perhaps the best-loved essential oil, calms. It's good for irritable children and, as mentioned above, also helps banish insomnia. Who among us doesn't love rose? Rose essential oil is pricey, just like jasmine and vanilla and some other rare essential oils. Rose is said to instill feelings of peace, happiness and love. And rose essential oil, unlike the modern, commercial bouquet of roses, does have a heavenly aroma where the bouquet doesn't, and a bottle of the oil won't wilt and die in a couple of days, either. The oil wins, hands down.

How to use essential oils and aromatherapy? You can add them to the bath, to massage oil, use as touch therapy by putting some on pulse points like wrists (some essential oils like cinnamon are strong and need to be diluted with a carrier oil before being placed on the skin) or you can mix them into your moisturizer.

I make my own toner to spray on my face before applying moisturizer. I simply put good water into a spray bottle and add a few drops of oil like geranium. Geranium, said to bring a glow to "mature" skin (!) is reported to also balance hormones, prevent mood swings and nervous tension. It's terrific in the summer to keep away bugs, including ticks. I drench myself before I go out into the garden.

I love to sprinkle the essential oils onto a piece of cloth and put that somewhere in the room, sprinkle them onto a rug (I do this all the time to my oriental rugs), or put them in a bowl of hot water or other source of heat, like a candle or electric diffuser. Here's a recipe for a therapeutic air freshener to diffuse however you like: 1 drop bergamot, 1 drop lemon, 1 drop geranium, 1 drop clary sage, 1 drop basil. Can you double, triple the recipe? Of course.

In France, aromatherapy is often prescribed by physicians, sold in pharmacies and covered by health insurance. In our country we pretty much have to learn on our own. I've found that experimenting is great fun. So, go to. Let your nose be your guide!

This next article has always been one of my favorites just because I thought I made a convincing argument to stop demonizing salt! Since its publication, good salts sell briskly in our store.

A Pinch of Salt? 2013

I've been wondering for years whether salt, whose overall intake has maintained steady despite all the warnings (if it's not in our packaged food, we're adding it ourselves at the table), is really bad for us, or whether it's just the refined salt that has done us in. Does the kind of salt we add to our food make a difference?

Before we are born, we float in the womb in sole (so-lay), an ancient Celtic word for the watery-salty solution that comprises our bodily fluids. Those same Celtic ancients believed that sole came from the ocean and that we are all born from the same fluids arising from the same soul... Poetic, isn't it?

So, back to salt. Yes, we need it live, but it can also harm us when we use too much.

The question is, however, are all salts created equal, and do they act the same in our bodies? I'm no scientist, but I think regular old table salt does more harm than good, and that it's nothing like whole salt. Regular table salt has been "purified" and reduced to 99.9 percent sodium and chloride. All the eighty-plus balancing trace elements and minerals that are important to us have been removed. Salt is no longer real salt. To me, table salt doesn't even taste the same as real salt...

David Brownstein, MD, in *Shattering the Myths About One of Nature's Most Necessary Nutrients*, says "The chemicals used to remove the 'impurities' can include sulfuric acid or chlorine. All food-grade salt (refined salt) in the US must comply with the National Academy of Science's Food Chemicals Codex Sodium, Chloride Monograph (1996). Up to two percent of refined salt may contain anti-caking, free-flowing, or conditioning agents, which can be toxic to the body. These agents include sodium ferrocyanide, ammonium citrate and aluminum silicate."

Why do we even use salt in our food? Well, salt not only intensifies flavor and makes food taste better, it's important for food safety and preservation (it's an antimicrobial). Today manufacturers use table salt ("refined" salt as opposed to what I'm calling "real" salt) because it's cheap and ubiquitous. To me, refined salt is like white sugar, which is just sweet without all those wonderful flavor tones one gets in raw or coconut sugar, or honey or maple syrup. Table salt is salty without tonal flavors from the minerals that are stripped out.

Today we keep hearing that salt (but nobody says which kind) causes hypertension or high blood pressure. Many doctors tell us to throw away the saltshaker. Is there evidence to support this directive?

A review published by The Cochrane Collective in the *American Journal of Hypertension* in August 2011 noted that results of its analysis of research on sodium and disease "showed no strong evidence of any effect of salt reduction on cardiovascular disease morbidity in people with normal blood pressure." The other authors did not agree that reduction of salt was necessarily the best course of action. "Our review focuses on dietary advice and has not found robust evidence to support this approach."

Yet, on the other side of the aisle, "Dietary sodium intake among Canadian adults with and without hypertension," published in the journal *Chronic Diseases in Canada* (March 2011), stated that nearly 30 percent of hypertension among Canadian adults may be attributed to excess dietary sodium. This prompted them to conclude that "better approaches are needed to reduce sodium intake in hypertension patients, as well as the general population."

In a *Journal of American Medicine* paper by Michael H. Alderman, a hypertension expert at Albert Einstein College of Medicine, a low-salt diet was associated with better clinical outcomes in only five of the eleven studies he considered; in the rest, the people on the low-salt diet fared either the same or worse.

Again, which salt are the scientists talk about? None of the studies looked at the use of unrefined salt. None tested people who ate refined salt versus those who used unrefined salt. And it would be difficult to conduct such a study assuming we all eat out and eat convenience foods over which we have no control!

Remember all those 80 minerals that are stripped out of table salt? Well, every 10 years, the US government does an analysis of thousands of its citizens looking at various markers of health. One such marker has been mineral intake. This survey is known as the National Health and Nutrition Examination Survey (NHANES). Over the last 30 years, NHANES has found a correlation between inadequate levels of minerals and the presence of hypertension.

Could this have anything to do with the fact that table salt has been refined and stripped of minerals? What would happen if all salt used today suddenly were restored to its normal, natural form? If unrefined salts (such as Celtic, Himalayan, Redmond Real Salt, and all those salts that are different colors and flavors from smoky to spicy) have the trace minerals we need, wouldn't one make the assumption they might actually help prevent and treat hypertension?

There are books written about healing using real salts. Some recommend using ½ teaspoon of unrefined salt per day in two quarts of water and drinking that to help digestive illness, make the immune system work better, improve energy levels and brain function. One such book is *Salt Your Way to Health.*

Unrefined salt is great for brushing your teeth (I combine Redmond Real Salt from Central Utah's mineral-rich salt deposit from an ancient sea) with baking soda and keep the mixture in a jar). When used on my toothbrush, this homemade tooth powder balances pH in the mouth and works against gum bleeding, periodontal diseases, ulcers and bad breath.

Away from teeth and back to flavor, unrefined salt crystals, in addition to being different-colored, have different shapes too. And their different shapes change how we perceive the saltiness on our tongue. Smaller salt crystals allowed for 20 percent less sodium in a test potato chip without affecting consumer preference. Refined salt crystals are typically finer than real salts, which seems a vote in table salt's favor, but even so, taste testers found that because of their herbal, smoky, earthy flavors, 30 percent less of unrefined salt was needed to give food a "Wow!"

While the scientists duke it out and huge amounts of refined salt are given to humans and animals in studies to induce a hypertensive effect, I'm going to eat real, good salt. To me it's the issue of whole versus broken down and denatured (made unnatural so products look "pure," will keep longer on shelves, etc.). Whole wheat flour versus white flour. White sugar versus sugars that haven't been bleached or refined.

I'm going to eat real, good salt not only because it seems more natural to me, but because they have more complex and interesting flavors.

This article on raw apple cider vinegar also appeared in our local newspaper the *Concord Journal*, and the day the paper came out, our shop sold out of apple cider vinegar—all brands, all sizes, all bottles. The power of the press!

So Many Uses for Raw Apple Cider Vinegar, 2014

In 420 BCE Hippocrates used raw apple cider vinegar to clean wounds. Sung Tse, the 10th century creator of Chinese forensic medicine, advocated washing hands with a mixture of sulfur and raw vinegar to avoid infection during autopsies, and Roman soldiers mixed raw apple cider vinegar (RACV) with water and drank it as a strengthening and energizing tonic. So did Japanese samurai. (The addition of raw vinegar to drinking water killed infectious agents and made the water safe.)

In our own country, RACV was used to disinfect and speed up wound healing during the American Civil War and as late as WWI.

Then, in the late 1950s, a man by the name of D.C. Jarvis wrote his best-selling book *Folk Medicine: A Vermont Doctor's Guide to Good Health*. RACV featured large. Jarvis promoted RACV for acid indigestion and wrote that most people who think they suffer from acid indigestion don't, but instead lack sufficient hydrochloric acid. RACV in water before meals might be just what the doctor ordered!

What is raw apple cider vinegar? It's the old-fashioned, naturally fermented, unfiltered, unpasteurized vinegar with the "mother" still in it. The mother isn't pretty; it's stringy and sometimes gelatinous. It makes the vinegar cloudy. But it's the real deal and has enzymes which the clear pasteurized vinegars do not.

What are some ways you might want to try RACV? Well, do you have a sore throat? Mix one tablespoon raw apple cider vinegar in a big glass of warm water. Take a mouthful. Gargle and spit out. Take another mouthful and swallow. Take a mouthful and gargle and then spit out. Take another mouthful and swallow. Continue until the glass is empty. Do this every hour (a few hours are usually enough). Bye-bye sore throat. Really. And all for pennies.

Have a sprain or strain? Warm a cup of RACV and saturate a cloth. Apply to sprain five minutes every hour. Will you smell like a salad? Yes. Does it work? Also yes.

There are those who say that sipping two teaspoons of RACV in 16 ounces water helps with weight loss (it helps break down fat, they say). You can't tell that by me. I eat my weight in good fat every day, and no amount of vinegar can get around that!

Constipated? Dr. Jarvis said that starting the day off by drinking one to two tablespoons of RACV with the same amount of honey mixed together in water helps with that, and others say drinking RACV each day helps with allergies.

Webmd.com says that the effect of RACV on blood glucose levels is perhaps the best-researched and most promising of cider vinegar's possible health benefits. Several studies found that it may help lower glucose levels. For instance, one 2007 study of people with type two diabetes found that taking two tablespoons of RACV before bed lowered glucose levels in the morning by 4 to 6 percent.

Other reasons to use RACV? It helps extract calcium from the fruits, vegetables and meat it is mixed with, helping in the process of maintaining strong bones. It's rich in potassium, and potassium deficiency causes a variety of ailments including hair loss, weak fingernails, brittle teeth, sinusitis and a permanently running nose.

RACV contains malic acid which is very helpful in fighting fungal and bacterial infections. This acid also dissolves and gradually eliminates uric acid deposits that form around joints, helping relieve joint pains.

How do I start each morning? With a spoonful of RACV and liquid chlorophyll (that's another story for another day) in a mug of water. Tastes okay, and I'm convinced it's doing me good.

My mother taught me that symphytum should be taken only after the bone has been set or is in place. This is important!

I took high amounts of omega-3 fats to amplify the effect of the herbs and spices, to help reduce inflammation and to keep the blood thin so blood clots wouldn't become an issue. Years ago, an MD told me for any "itis" or inflammatory condition (arthritis, for instance), to take nine capsules of 1,200 mg fish oil a day for ten days–three capsules with each meal (always take with food, in the middle of the meal), then to back down to three to four capsules a day. That's what I did.

Collagen. Knowing that it is the most abundant protein in the human body and is the substance that holds the body together, I sipped bone broth or used collagen powder to make smoothies.

On the subject of smoothies: some days I used whey protein in an additional protein shake because there is evidence that whey protein stimulates bone-building osteoblast cells, too.

Other foods rich in collagen are canned salmon and sardines, as long as they have bones. Don't forget to eat other foods that help with healing: all the greens like kale, mustard greens, turnip greens, bok choy and broccoli. Eat foods such as nuts and seeds, seaweed and plain yogurt.

Boswellia serrata. Adam gave me this supplement (it's Indian Frankincense). I knew about it vaguely for joint pain, but now read that boswellia encourages formation of new blood vessels at the site of injury. I noticed the stiffness in my knees went away with it and the extra omega-3s.

BioSil. Silica aids in the flexibility of bone collagen matrix. According to the BioSil website, "in clinical trials, BioSil increased bone collagen formation 15 percent and increased BMD 2.00 percent at the critical hip region over and above what calcium and Vitamin D alone could do after one year."

Vitamin C, bioflavonoids and flavonols such as quercetin soothe the inflammatory process and speed healing. I was already taking vitamin C but upped the dose. You can eat your vitamin C by emphasizing fruits and vegetables such as citrus, bell peppers, strawberries and tomatoes.

Adam handed me a formula by Solaray called Deep Vein Support that contains bromelain, horse chestnut and butcher's broom. I took it because deep vein thrombosis (when blood clots in your veins can break loose and travel through your bloodstream) is a concern when one doesn't move for a long time, and in my case I was assigned bed rest for some weeks.

Vitamins K2 and D3. I was already taking these but doubled my dose. Vitamin D, in conjunction with vitamin K, stimulates the transformation of fracture site stem cells to bone building osteoblasts. Overall, vitamin D is central to fracture healing and vitamin D status has been shown to be an independent predictor of functional recovery after hip fracture.

Magnesium. I always take magnesium glycinate, which helps my body absorb calcium from my diet (I haven't taken calcium supplements for a number of years now). Many of you have heard me say that as long as I take magnesium glycinate, I don't get leg cramps. The magnesium helps my vitamin D work, and since this is a part of building and maintaining healthy bones, I continued with it, of course!

I ate carefully the first two months. Then I fell off the wagon with dessert. But I used those pH testing strips on my tongue to make sure I was mostly alkaline, around seven, to provide a healing environment for bones and bod. That means I ate lots of steamed greens dressed with good fat over whole grains or lentils. I fell in love with eggs all over again.

Acidic foods/drinks and sugar can cause bones to break down over time if not buffered by foods that are more alkaline such as greens, green juice, avocados, sweet potatoes or bananas.

Avoid highly acidic drinks like colas, diet sodas, coffee, black tea, cranberry juice and alcohol. Potassium is your new best friend. Green tea is less acidic than coffee.

Zinc. Normally, I take a zinc picolinate capsule every day. When I broke my ankle, I increased the daily amount of zinc to 60 mg. The chemical reactions necessary to rebuild the bone require zinc. Try nibbling pumpkin seeds which are especially rich in zinc and have protein and good fats.

My plan is not to fall on black ice, ever again. May you never break a bone, but if you do, may you recover quickly!

I always wish I'd written an article on potatoes, a food that has gotten an undeserved bad rap.

Potatoes, eaten in their jackets, are satisfying and good food. I like an olive-oily potato salad with lots of dill and chopped onion. I like potatoes baked or steamed and mashed with cooked carrots and parsnips. Mashed with grass-fed butter and flaky sea salt. And I like to try all different kinds of potatoes. I grow purple potatoes.

Years ago, *The Natural Foods Merchandiser*, one of our trade magazines, had a column by Mark Mulcahy who is an organic produce expert, wrote an article called "Regular Spuds are Environmental Duds!" He said that every time we buy a standard potato like an Idaho or russet, we are contributing to the loss of biodiversity because of the 235 known species of potatoes, we use basically just four in the US.

Remember the Irish potato famine of 1845-46? One and a half million people died, and one million more left Ireland. The severity of the blight was generally attributed to reliance on the lumper potato which had no resistance to disease. Well, we are now experiencing resurgence of late blight in the US potato growing regions because these four limited potato varieties aren't bred for blight resistance. Conventional farmers rely on chemicals, even though the blight is resistant to most pesticides.

Mark says we've made the disease stronger and the potato weaker by limiting the diversity of potatoes we grow. He's suggesting we stock heirlooms, fingerlings, purple and other varieties of potatoes. My tidbit here is to seeks these out!

FYI–potatoes like to sprout, as we know. To stifle this urge, conventional potato packers use sprout inhibitors such as Sprout Nip, which carries a "danger" warning on its label and has the EPA's highest grade for toxicity.

To help prevent organic potatoes from sprouting, store in a cool, dark place–the fridge is okay. But let potatoes warm up before using because the cold changes starch to sugar and warming them changes it back again. Did you know this? I didn't!

I'm not sure why I'm stuck on potatoes here. Let me end the potato saga with another story. Up until the 16th century the French believed potatoes caused leprosy. Antoine-Augustin Parmantier, who was French and a prisoner of the Prussians during the Seven Years War, ate many a potato. Upon release, he convinced the French they were missing out.

My grandma Sarah, from Poland, told me that similarly, the tomato was considered poisonous back in the old country. She ate her first tomato in New York City and lived to tell the tale.

To end the tale of potatoes, here's one of my favorite potato salad recipes from our July 2018 store newsletter:

My Mother's Potato Salad

Mom always used extra virgin olive oil and garlic in her potato salads. The best! Yes, take on a picnic. Serve with whatever you have on the grill. This is Summer heaven. Please do use Les Moulins Mahjoub capers because they are what capers are meant to be. You will love them!

Serves 4-6   **Use organic ingredients, of course.**

6 medium-sized red-skin potatoes	2 Tbsp Les Moulins Mahjoub capers
½ C extra virgin olive oil	½ C finely chopped fresh dill*
2 large garlic cloves, pressed	1 C pitted, Nicoise olives**
¾ C chopped onion	1 tsp good salt and black pepper

1 C crumbled feta or goat cheese	4 hard-boiled eggs, peeled and
3 Tbsp red wine vinegar	quartered lengthwise
	¼ C pitted Nicoise olives, garnish

Scrub potatoes. Put in pot with water and simmer, covered, until tender, about 20 minutes. Drain, cool until you can hold and cut into bite-sized pieces (don't worry about skin–you want that rustic look). In a bowl, toss potatoes with extra virgin olive oil and garlic. Cool potatoes to room temperature. Then add onion, feta or goat cheese. Drizzle with vinegar. Add remaining ingredients. Toss gently. Allow Mom's potato salad to sit for an hour. Garnish with remaining olives and have a party!

*If you don't have fresh dill, dried dill weed works, but use more. **You can find pitted Nicoise olives in our refrigerated produce case. This salad keeps for several days in the fridge but bring to room temp before eating.*

• •

There are so many tidbits about kale, which also stars on TV as a scapegoat for inedible. About ten years ago, *Mother Earth News* dubbed kale "the new star of leafy greens" in a piece entitled "33 Greatest Foods for Healthy Living," giving it top marks for nutrient density, flavor and availability.

Today, this is old hat. But did you know who the largest consumer of kale is in our country? Fast food joints like Pizza Hut and McDonalds, where it is used for decorating salad bars. Isn't that an interesting tidbit?

A newsletter written for the Moscow Food Coop in Moscow, Idaho, said that "while kale's inner beauty may be underappreciated here, that appears not to be the case in Europe, where it has grown since around 600 B.C.E. and was, until the end of the Middle Ages, the most common green vegetable. In northern Germany many communities have yearly kale festivals complete with the crowning of a kale king."

"In Scotland," Wikipedia says, "kale provided such a base for a traditional diet that the word in some Scots dialects is synonymous with food. To be 'off one's kail' is to feel too ill to eat. In Ireland, kale is mixed with mashed potatoes to make the traditional dish called colcannon. It's popular on Halloween, when it may be served with sausages."

A final tidbit from my mom: sprinkle chicken with turmeric powder before putting it in the oven because turmeric kills e coli. How did she know that in the fifties? Who first suggested using curry powder thousands of years ago (one of the ingredients in curry powder is turmeric) to keep food safe?

Completely opposite to historical food safety, this newsfeed was sent to me by brother, David:

> Within squealing distance of the Hogway Speedway, nothing seems more apropos than a snout full of fried food. And the North Carolina Mountain State Fair provides an embarrassment of battered riches. Fried Oreos, for instance, are one of the biggest things to emerge from the deep-fat fryer this year. A careful deep-frying renders them pillowy-soft and creamy, though the obligatory blanket of powdered sugar renders

them too cloying to eat too many, unless your sweet tooth is particularly powerful.

And the article goes on and on and on about things like fried pop tarts then dusted with powdered sugar.

Only in America. And only in America do people order double cheeseburgers, large fries, and *a diet* coke. Only in America can a pizza get to your house faster than an ambulance. And those are the reasons I spout my tidbits and Adam and I write our newsletter columns!

Chapter 15

What Are My Top Foods And Supplements?

I get asked all the time what my favorite foods are. I get asked what supplements I take, as if what I take as grandma bear is right for papa bear, mama bear and baby bear. My porridge is just right, for me. But because it would be churlish to say, "It's none of your business!", here are my lists, some of my favorites and why.

Keep in mind, however, as you read my supplement list, that I'm no longer a spring chicken (think: do your ears hang low, can you swing them to and fro) and I've added supplements that have to do with aging, for my eyes, for my brain and for my joints.

My favorite supplements. Sometimes people poke through my basket at the checkout counter wanting to see what I buy. Here *in brief* because volumes can be written about each, are my favorite vitamins. *I also take homeopathics and use food as medicine.* Do I take vitamins every day? No. There are times I simply can't bear the sight of another vitamin and I stop cold turkey for a few days. Years ago, Rick Scalzo of Gaia Herbs suggested we take supplements six days and stop on the seventh. I like the idea of a day of rest. I like that I get to be lazy one day a week. And it makes sense that our body, as well as our mind, deserves some down-time.

I don't take a multivitamin because I take so many things individually. I like to tinker, to vary my regimen. That's my choice. Yours might be to go the route of a multi and skip most everything else. A good multivitamin/mineral does fill nutritional holes, just like rotating the tires on your car will prevent undue wear and tear in one spot on your tires. A multi will protect against diseases of scarcity like scurvy or rickets. That's what they're for. Here's what I take:

Vitamin C with bioflavonoids

A ten-year 1992 UCLA study involving 11,000 Americans found that vitamin C increased life span. Deaths from cardiovascular disease were reduced by 40 percent. In a 12-year study conducted by Harvard scientists, women who used vitamin C for ten years or more lowered their risk of developing cataracts by 45 percent.

Studies done in the 1930s and 1940s revealed that subjects with the highest blood levels of vitamin C had the lowest blood pressure, that vitamin C given in large doses to cancer patients was often effective and non-toxic, that taking vitamin C daily keeps hearts strong and protects diabetics. High glucose levels *compete* with vitamin C, making more C necessary. And yes, vitamin C can stop the common cold in its tracks if you act quickly and take plenty.

Vitamin E (plus tocotrienols)

A report in *JAMA* confirmed that vitamin E dramatically slows the progression of heart disease, and that taking vitamin E before surgery improved chances of survival. According to a study in *Lancet*, non-fatal heart attacks were reduced by an astounding 77 percent after patients took 400 i.u. of vitamin E daily for 200 days.

Vitamin E is said to retard cellular and mental aging. It oxygenates tissues, which makes wounds and burns heal more quickly. It improves skin problems and texture. The National Institute on Aging found that people over 75 who took vitamin E were 43 percent less apt to die over a nine-year period than those who did not. Taking E and C together prolongs the good life.

Alpha Lipoic Acid

Also known as "lipoic acid", alpha lipoic acid (ALA) is just about my favorite antioxidant because it works in both the fat and water cells. It regenerates and recirculates other antioxidants like vitamin C and E. Nowadays, I take Systemic C by Source Naturals, because that formula includes ALA and grape seed extract together with C.

ALA helps produce the immune-protective antioxidant enzyme glutathione, and it helps regulate blood sugar levels, which is why I hear Grace, our nurse, suggesting its use by her diabetic patients. ALA is found in foods like meats and spinach, medically approved in Germany for treating adult-onset type two diabetes.

CoQ10

CoQ10 is a vitamin-like substance found in every cell in the body and responsible for 95 percent of all cellular energy. An Italian study reported that 80 percent of 1,100 patients with heart failure improved after taking CoQ10. In Japan CoQ10 is used in the treatment of heart disease and high blood pressure and to enhance the immune system. Japanese studies have also found that CoQ10 may help heal duodenal ulcers, counter histamine and help allergy and asthma sufferers. CoQ10 has been shown to increase physical performance.

I heard Dr. Stephen Sinatra, a cardiologist, speak once at Natural Products Expo East, and he said if he had to put his heart patients on only one thing besides a good multi, it would be CoQ10. Some common heart drugs aggravate a CoQ10 deficiency. Lovastatin, for example, lowers cholesterol levels but also inhibits the body's production of CoQ10.

Carotenoids (Astaxanthin)

Carotenoids are essential for healthy vision, immunity, wound-healing and more. Carotenoids are said to maintain cell structure and integrity, to keep skin moist and elastic, and to help prevent infection.

My favorite carotenoid is astaxanthin, which is found in marine life such as micro-algae, krill, salmon and crustaceans. Fat soluble, astaxanthin is able to cross the blood brain/eye barrier so it can go to work better. The fact that Ironman Champion Dave Scott swears by it for recovery, too, is good enough for me!

Years ago, we had a speaker at the store who said if she could afford one supplement only for her eyes, she'd choose astaxanthin. Astaxanthin is my foundational supplement for eye health.

Co-Enzyme B vitamins and Brewer's or Nutritional Yeast

I take a co-enzyme B complex morning and evening. I try and make sure I get some brewer's or nutritional yeast in my diet as well because it's a rich source of the B vitamins (the nerve and stress vitamins).

B vitamins are used to regulate glucose, to aid in the treatment of wounds, to treat burns and help alleviate skin problems. They maintain muscle tone and promote good liver function. B vitamins are involved in energy production and may be useful in the treatment of depression or anxiety.

I put brewer's yeast in a smoothie or sprinkle some on a salad. I also blend two cups brewer's yeast with two cups walnuts or cashews (or another nut or seed) and one tablespoon good salt. I store this in my freezer and use with gay abandon. It tastes just like Parmesan cheese; I kid you not.

Note that Brewer's and nutritional yeast are not *the type of yeast which causes yeast infections and they can be taken if you are treating a yeast infection (candida albicans).*

Good Fats

I take fish oil, krill oil, borage oil and black seed oil, all because they help with everything under the sun. Not only does my skin benefit (vain creature that I am), but my heart and joints and dry eyes are improved, too. Fats are vital for neurological health, and they enhance cognitive function and decrease the risk of heart disease. They definitely are anti-inflammatory.

Magnesium Glycinate

I tell everyone that it's been years since I've supplemented with calcium. I truly believe that our American diet has plenty of calcium, but that we have trouble absorbing it because we don't get enough good magnesium and vitamin D, which are needed for calcium absorption.

Magnesium is also essential for effective nerve and muscle functioning, converts blood sugar into energy, aids in fighting depression, promotes cardiovascular health, helps prevent kidney and gallstones and brings relief from indigestion. It relaxes the muscles. Get leg cramps? Try taking a good magnesium.

By good magnesium, I don't mean magnesium oxide which is the least absorbable. That's why people who are constipated take magnesium oxide as a laxative. It just moves right through you!

I like magnesium glycinate, but there are other good magnesiums out there, too.

Anti-Aging Supplements, things I play with

I won't know until I'm dying whether the anti-aging supplements have made a difference, but some I play with are a) Niagen, which received the FDA's new dietary ingredient status to "Age Better." It fuels the body's mitochondria; b) Collagen and Hyaluronic Acid (HA), which are supposed to help prevent wrinkles and keep joints healthier; c) Boswellia, known as *Indian frankincense*. It's an herbal extract used for centuries in Asian and African folk medicine to treat chronic inflammatory illnesses, as well as a number of other health conditions; d) I use Hawthorne to keep my heart healthy; and finally, e) I use colloidal silver to spray a sore throat and to take by the teaspoon when I feel something coming on.

Top Foods for Health and Happiness!

Here are some of my favorite foods for keeping healthy, wealthy and wise. Each New Year I ask myself if I'm making them a part of my diet. If I'm not, I try to work them in again.

Almonds. Did you know that a fifth of an almond's weight is pure protein? Almonds contain vitamin E, which helps keep hearts healthy. An Australian study found men who eat three ounces of almonds a day for three weeks cut cholesterol by ten percent. Cancer clinics around the world recommend ten almonds a day, and Loma Linda University made the startling discover a number of years ago that people who make nuts and seeds a part of a balanced diet are less likely to be obese than those who go the fat-free route. Have you ever tried tamari-roasted almonds? Yum.

Bee pollen and royal jelly. Royal jelly is the food fed to one worker bee, who then turns into the queen bee. The queen bee not only grows bigger, but lives much longer.

Bee products are a complete protein because they have all the amino acids, and royal jelly is used by athletes for endurance and stamina. Bee food contains hydroxy decanoic acid which kills E. coli and salmonella bacteria. They exert a radioprotective effect and are used to help heal wounds and minimize wrinkles.

My favorite way to get bee food is in honey, which contains royal jelly and bee pollen (available at natural food stores; the brand we carry is YSBee). When I get up in the morning, I drink my glass of water with liquid chlorophyll and raw apple cider vinegar and then have my spoonful of YSBee honey with royal jelly and bee pollen and propolis (another bee product–propolis is the black stuff bees paint around the entrance to their hives which prevents them from bringing germs inside). I love this thick, sweet treat, and I love scraping the spoon off with my teeth.

Green tea. *Camellia sinensis* has been used medicinally in China for over 4,000 years. Today we know green tea contains polyphenolic catechins, said to be powerful antioxidants with cancer-fighting capabilities, which also have been found to not only protect our cells but to support the body's immune system and reduce the risk of stroke and cardiovascular disease. In addition to helping us stay younger longer, Japanese studies have shown green tea can lower blood pressure, reduce bad cholesterol and keep blood sugar levels from rising inappropriately.

Some studies say more frequent consumption of green tea results in people who are happier because it contains the amino acid l-theanine, which is thought to have a soothing, calming effect on the brain. Green tea also inhibits dental plaque and cavity formation, and it inhibits many food-borne bacteria.

With regard to blood pressure, researchers speculate that green tea lowers blood pressure by causing blood vessels to relax. One study that compared more than 50 vegetables, fruits, nuts, herbs, spices and teas for their ability to relax blood vessels, found that green tea placed fifth, relaxing blood vessel walls by as much as 91 percent.

Hot peppers contain capsaicin which prevents carcinogens from binding to DNA. Raw oysters and clams are always offered with hot sauce perhaps because hot peppers kill harmful bacteria. Putting hot sauce on food speeds up metabolism and improves digestion. Contrary to public opinion, hot peppers don't hurt the stomach or promote ulcers. If you suffer from cold hands or feet, try eating hot peppers, because they also get the circulation going. Who doesn't need improved circulation? Keep a jar of cayenne handy to jazz up even cottage cheese!

Kale. The Center for Science in the Public Interest rated kale high up there among vegetables in terms of total nutrients. Kale is called "king of calcium" and like other members of the cruciferous family helps prevent cancer. It contains phytonutrients which help regulate estrogen, too. I've gotten to love kale. Just chop it up stem and all, steam in a little water for five minutes, dress with olive oil and lemon juice. Add ginger or garlic. Kale works well in soups and is a wonderful accompaniment to pasta.

Garlic was used in ancient Egypt to build strength. Today we know it not only wards off vampires, lowers serum cholesterol and blood pressure and helps prevent heart attacks and strokes. Garlic also appears to lift mood and is a good cold medication. What's a pasta sauce or salad dressing without lots and lots of garlic?

In 2014, Robin Cherry wrote in *Bon Appetit* magazine: "Garlic's health benefits have been touted throughout history, and it's been credited as a plague-beating, infection-fighting, fat-melting, parasite-killing, cholesterol-lowering, immune-system-boosting, cancer-preventing, bronchitis-curing, blood pressure-controlling, impotence-treating, ringworm-healing, strength-building, mosquito-repelling cure-all that improves digestion, circulation, respiratory health and fertility. And that's just a partial list."

Shiitake mushrooms are rated number one on an ancient Chinese list of superior medicines. Touted as a substance to give eternal youth and longevity, shiitakes contain a virus that produces interferon, which fights cancer. They are used to treat hepatitis B and cirrhosis and work well at healing the liver. Nowadays, you can always get fresh shiitakes. Sauté in butter and olive oil together with garlic, salt and pepper. Serve alongside the entrée or as a special appetizer. You can also toss shiitakes with pesto and roast them in the oven.

Fermented and cultured foods. Fermented foods are rich in good bacteria, probiotics that help our gut, improve digestion, boost immunity and help us maintain a healthy weight. Every culture around the world has its version of fermented foods, like yogurt and kimchi, sauerkraut, miso, tempeh and more. It's not hard putting a forkful of cultured veggies on a dinner plate or adding two tablespoons of miso to a bowl of soup.

Sweet potatoes and yams. "If you want a good jolt of beta carotene, the substance that seems to protect against heart disease and cancer, simply eat sweet potatoes," says nutritionist Jean Carper. They have lots of fiber and are easy for the body to digest when you're stressed. Try a couple of baked sweets for breakfast with some nut or seed butter.

Sesame butter (just like peanut butter but from sesame seeds, aka tahini). Sesame products are eaten in some cultures in place of dairy products because of their high calcium content (calcium from sesame seeds is more easily used by our bodies than calcium from milk). Another quick and easy breakfast is apple slices dipped into sesame butter, or sesame butter put on banana, banana-split style. Try sesame butter on toast. Use to replace peanut butter in cookies.

Important to note, however, that the health benefits from sesame butter or tahini are in whole sesame tahini, made from whole sesame seeds with the hulls. Once those hulls are removed, you lose nutrients. It's like eating white bread.

Seeds. There are so many seeds, which is delightful. Try tiny chia seeds, which are a high-energy endurance food. Aztec runners used chia to sustain themselves. Hemp seeds contain easily digestible protein and are a rich source of essential fatty acids, phytosterols, carotenes, vitamin E and vitamin C and chlorophyll. And 35 percent of hemp is dietary fiber. How does hemp taste? Like sunflower seeds. Did you know the oldest printed paper in existence is a 100 percent hemp Chinese text dated 770 AD, or that Thomas Jefferson drafted the Declaration of Independence *and* our Constitution on hemp paper?

Lentils give us protein, have cholesterol-lowering fiber, and more nutrition for their size than almost any other food. Do they contain iron and B vitamins? Yes! These cute little pulses (aka lentils) come in all colors and are easy on the pocketbook, too. A few feed many. Want to whittle down your waist? Lentils will play a starring role.

Eggs. I suggest eggs whenever someone asks about protein. Eggs are a pretty near darn perfect food. A study published in the *Journal of Nutrition* some years back said eating an egg a day helps prevent age-related macular degeneration, the leading cause of vision loss among those of us over 50. That's because eggs contain lutein, an antioxidant critical to eye health, and people can absorb lutein from eggs more easily than from any other dietary source.

My mother was a firm believer in eggs. "They're one of nature's super-foods!" She kept eating them and giving them to us even when doctors declared them a public health hazard. She marched to her own drummer.

I want to end this on a humorous note, and I will. I really wanted to leave you with humor by Harry Golden, who wrote "Only in America," but instead below are some jokes suitable for small children.

Q: Why did the Orange go out with a Prune? A: Because he couldn't find a Date!

Q: Why did the students eat their homework? A: Because the teacher said that it was a piece of cake.

Q: What did the burger name her daughter? A: Patty!

Q: What do you get if you divide the circumference of a jack-o-lantern by its diameter? A: Pumpkin pi.

Q: Why couldn't the sesame seed leave the casino? A: Because he was on a roll.

Chapter 16

The End: What's The Future?

I don't know if it's even worth trying to picture the future. It's like science fiction. It's all imaginary and beyond that. Who can know where technology will take us? Will drones deliver not only packages but employees to work? Will food turn into pills like in the Woody Allen movie Sleeper?

Modern food is already here. Read what Adam wrote in 2009:

Homogenized Plastic Mass: It's What's For Dinner

I'm not completely opposed to junk food. For example, the occasional leftover French fry scavenged from the plate of a dining companion, or the deep fat-fried Snickers-bar-on-a-stick at Redbone's in Davis Square, Somerville. Those, I feel, are worth it.

But for the most part, I just wonder why. I mean, really, why eat most of the crap that's out there? Having been raised on good food, I'm constantly amazed that people would crave, say, a Fenway Frank over the much-more-delicious Niman organic hot dog. Or a white-flour-Crisco-crusted corn syrup Cool Whip pie over something with whole grains and actual fruit and soaring peaks of whipped cream. For the most part, natural–which is to say "real"–just tastes better.

Nowhere is this truer than when it comes to cheese. I love cheese. I respect cheese. I write love sonnets to cheese, in all its cheesy beauty. So, you can imagine how shocked and offended I was when, for the first time in my more than thirty years, my taste buds experienced the Day-Glo dairy mucous extrusion that's splotched over lukewarm tortilla chips & called "nachos" at a movie theater.

What is this industrial waste?

That's not a rhetorical question! What exactly is nacho spread made of? To answer that question, here's an excerpt from the US Code of Federal Regulations, Title 21: Food and Drugs.

Part 133—CHEESES AND RELATED CHEESE PRODUCTS
Subpart B—Requirements for Specific Standardized Cheeses and Related Products

§ 133.179 Pasteurized process cheese spread.

(a)(1) Pasteurized process cheese spread is the food prepared by comminuting and mixing, with the aid of heat, one or more of the optional cheese ingredients prescribed in paragraph (c) of this section, with or without one or more of the optional dairy ingredients prescribed in paragraph (d) of this section, with one or more of the emulsifying agents prescribed in paragraph (e) of this section, and with or without one or more of the optional ingredients prescribed by paragraph (f) of this section, into a homogeneous plastic mass, which is spreadable at 70° F.

...then follow a few paragraphs involving advanced dairy mathematics...

(a)(6) The weight of each variety of cheese in a pasteurized process cheese spread made with two varieties of cheese is not less than 25 percent of the total weight of both, except that the weight of blue cheese, nuworld cheese, Roquefort cheese, gorgonzola cheese, or limburger cheese is not less than 10 percent of the total weight of both...."

Adam says if we want to read more, we can find it online at http://ecfr.gpoaccess.gov. He also says that we could probably find "hot dog" on there as well. "But, really," he asks, "why give yourself nightmares?"

Our shop is fighting for real food, for a community that treasures what is authentic. I see the future as two steps forward and three steps backward. The farming movement and slow food will create a hunger for what's real in the best sense of the word, while right alongside come the processed food folks seeking respectability. I see kids so allergic to anything true that all they can eat is fake food.

My mission, and the mission of our shop? To jump up and down. To support farmers in their efforts to restore soil health. To put in our own home gardens. To use neem and soapy water instead of pesticides to keep bugs at bay. To carry this theme to every part of our life.

The future is fragile and needs our help. I want a future where people listen to one another. Where conversation is thoughtful and has large doses of humor.

Let's none of us settle for anything less. And since this book is about coming together and food, I want a future where we are interested in each other whether we be omnivores, carnivores, vegans, Paleo or any other isms that may come along. I want a world where we feel pleasure as we bite into a pear and taste its sweetness.

But really, what am I going to do? I'm going to breathe in and breathe out, confident that our shop will thrive as long as there are human beings, because we need places where we can look another human being in the eye to balance the rushing race forward of technology. Despite the excitement of "progress," there will always be hunger for comfort and connection.

Our final chapter is not written. Today we all ooh and ahh about leeks, swear by CBD and breathe in cardamom, clary sage and cedarwood. And we inhale the aroma of garlic and ginger from the kitchen's oven. We lift one another up. That's worth a bushel and a peck, don't you think?

Recently, one of our young staffers, Gregoria, died. It was unexpected. It shook us. Gregoria's husband told us how much Gregoria loved being in our shop. She cherished, he said, being with all of us, and that "all of us" included our staff and darling customers. And when I looked back, I saw that almost every photo I'd taken of the Early Bird pajama party and of the store's birthday party celebrations after Gregoria came to Debra's Natural Gourmet, pictured her laughing.

I remember her grammatical errors because English was not her native tongue. "I'm not agree with you," she would say. And I still use the pen she brought back for me from Bolivia with a hat on top. Pens on my desk have always, forever, gone missing. When Gregoria handed me this gift, she promised no one would walk off with it. She was right.